GIRLS

Will PUBERTY Last My Whole Life?

REAL Answers to REAL Questions
from Preteens About Body Changes, Sex,
and Other Growing-Up Stuff

· ·

Julie Metzger, RN, MN, and Robert Lehman, MD

Illustrated by Lia Cerizo

little bigfoot

an imprint of sasquatch books
seattle, wa

Manufactured in China by C&C Offset Printing Co. Ltd. Shenzhen, Guangdong Province, in April 2018

Published by Little Bigfoot, an imprint of Sasquatch Books

22 21 20 19 18   9 8 7 6 5 4 3 2 1

Editor: Susan Roxborough | Production editor: Em Gale
Copyeditor: Jessyca Murphy | Design: Anna Goldstein

Library of Congress Cataloging-in-Publication Data
Names: Metzger, Julie Giesy, author. | Lehman, Robert, 1952- author. |
   Cerizo, Lia, illustrator.
Title: Will puberty last my whole life? : real answers to real questions from
   preteens about body changes, sex, and other growing-up stuff / Julie
   Metzger, RN, MN, and Robert Lehman, MD ; illustrated by Lia Cerizo.
Description: Revised edition. | Seattle, WA : Little Bigfoot, an imprint of
   Sasquatch Books, [2018] | Includes bibliographical references and index.
   Identifiers: LCCN 2017061514 | ISBN 9781632171795 (paperback : alk. paper)
Subjects: LCSH: Puberty--Juvenile literature. | Teenage
   girls--Physiology--Juvenile literature. | Teenage
   boys--Physiology--Juvenile literature. | Interpersonal relations in
   adolescence--Juvenile literature.
   Classification: LCC QP84.4 .M48 2018 | DDC 612.6/61--dc23
   LC record available at https://lccn.loc.gov/2017061514

ISBN: 978-1-63217-179-5

SASQUATCH BOOKS
1904 Third Avenue, Suite 710 | Seattle, WA 98101
(206) 467-4300 | SasquatchBooks.com

Contents

Introduction

Welcome to the book of questions on puberty, sex, and other growing-up stuff asked by preteen girls (and boys too—flip the book over to see the boys' side)!

Who is asking these questions, you might wonder? Every single question in this book has been written on a note card by someone *just like you*. For more than thirty years Julie Metzger (me) and Rob Lehman (who answers the boys' questions), along with our amazing colleagues, have been talking to preteens (along with trusted adults) in a class called Great Conversations, where we discuss important ideas about growing up. (Wow! That is a *lot* of classes and a *lot* of questions!)

In our classes we have conversations about what happens as our bodies change from looking and working like kid bodies to looking and working like adult bodies (a process called puberty), about how we make decisions in friendships and relationships, and all about sex, sexuality, gender identity, and babies. We invite kids, mostly ten- to twelve-year-olds, to ask a question on a note card so we can answer them for the whole group. *This book is a collection* of the questions that are asked the most. It also features some of our favorites sprinkled in and some that really helped everyone understand what is on the minds of preteens. Being curious and getting information about other people's experiences—what happens to different bodies, what others worry and think about—helps all of us understand the *human being experience*. Although each of us has our own journey of growing up, much of what happens to us also happens to other human beings! Hopefully after reading this book you will have information that will help you make healthy decisions about your body and your relationships.

We hope you will share some of the questions and answers with your parents, teachers, or anyone else interested in what might be on your mind and the minds of other kids. We know that parents and other trusted adults in your life are some of the most important resources you have—and they *want* this whole growing-up thing to go well for you! Our answers are not meant to tell the whole story or be the final word— *just the opposite*. We hope this is the beginning of more Great Conversations.

Thank you to the families who come to our classes, for being **brave** enough to ask questions and **curious** enough to keep the conversation going. And to our astonishing colleagues who work with us at Great Conversations, who continually raise the bar on communicating with families on important things.

My deepest gratitude for my parents, Jerry and PR, for their lifetime of advocacy for me and for so many others; to Michael, for his enduring love and support; and to Peter, Roxanne, Kathryn, and Emma, for their daily inspiration. I am so proud of your work as grown-ups talking to young people about important things.

Julie

JULIE GIESY METZGER, RN, MN

Julie Metzger, RN, MN, has worked for more than thirty years with families of preteens and teens on topics of puberty, sexuality, and decision-making. Bringing a wealth of knowledge from her experiences, she is a well-respected and popular speaker on a wide range of parenting issues, has worked in many capacities as a nurse consultant, and is the parent of three young adults. Julie has also written and presented health curricula on decision-making and friendships for middle and high school students and advocated for adolescents and families in the community. For more information on classes, programs, and other resources, visit GreatConversations.com.

great **conversations**
about growing up. together.

1. When You Are All Grown Up, Do You Wish You Were a Kid?

. . . And Other Questions About Growing Up

What is the POINT of puberty?

Puberty is the time when your body **changes** from looking and working like a kid's body into **an adult body**. The whole process usually starts for girls sometime in elementary school, continues through middle school, and finishes up when you are a teenager in high school—but, everybody's timing is uniquely their own! The message to begin this whole process starts in our brain, which sends hormones (chemicals we can't see) to different body parts. *Most girls* are born with body parts like vaginas and uteruses, with hormones called estrogen and progesterone (and a little bit of testosterone). Puberty will look different for most boys who have body parts like penises and testicles, and the hormone testosterone, which sends messages about their puberty experience. However, lots of what happens in puberty is similar for *everyone*. You will most likely get pimples and body odor (sometimes called B.O.); your body will get taller, put on weight, change shape; and your voice will change. You will become more *aware of your feelings*, and you will most likely become interested in relationships with other people. The entire transformation takes several years, and when it is finished you pretty much look like a **grown-up**. Have you ever been curious about what boys experience in puberty? It might be surprising to learn how much of puberty is similar and the interesting ways it is different. Learning about what boys **wonder and worry** about gives you information that can be helpful about your own experience, and can help give you empathy for people with different experiences, which makes for healthy bodies *and* relationships. **Flip** this book over and check out their questions and the answers!

. . . .

Do ALL GIRLS have puberty?

Each girl has their own unique experience of puberty—different in some way than all other girls. *And at the same time* each girl will share many parts of puberty with every other girl in the world—including all girls who have lived in the past and all girls who will live in the future. That's *a lot* of girls! Some girls start puberty earlier, some finish later, but most people with girls' bodies experience the basics, including growing taller, gaining weight, growing breasts, getting pimples and body odor, growing hair in new and interesting places, and having periods. There are lots of reasons we have **differences** in our puberty experience from others. One big reason is that we receive messages from our birth parents that influence our experience of puberty. Birth parents determine lots of things about us—our skin color, whether our hair is curly or straight. Birth parents also influence how fast we go through puberty or how slow, whether we start puberty earlier than our friends or later, and the size and shape we ultimately become. We all have **unique** bodies— sometimes our body parts work differently; sometimes we take medicine that changes our puberty experience; sometimes we have a condition that makes us different than other people. When you consider all that, it means every person has unique attributes that make their puberty experience their very own.

Why can't puberty just happen to SOME of us?

When kids hear about puberty, they sometimes wish they could skip the whole thing—for some kids, *nothing* about it sounds interesting! Actually some of the fun is going through it all right along with your friends. Even though everyone's experience will be uniquely their own, much of what you experience will be the same as everyone else. And the end result is having a grown-up body and brain ready to be an adult. As your body and brain change, you'll have plenty of time to practice some of the important work of being a grown-up.

. . . .

When WILL all this happen for me?

Although *puberty for most girls* starts with an increase in height and weight, lots of girls don't notice that puberty has begun since they have been busy *growing their whole lives*! Many girls first notice they have started puberty when they begin to develop breasts—this is the first *new* body change of puberty for most girls (for much more about breasts, turn to page 23). Girls typically *start* puberty sometime between the ages of eight and eleven. It's not uncommon for girls to begin puberty up to *two years* before boys!

. . . .

Will puberty happen to me like other girls? I don't feel very GIRLISH.

Your puberty experience is largely determined by your body parts and hormones, which is your *biological sex*. Being labeled "a girl" or "a boy" is our *gender*. Gender is more than reproductive body parts—it's a mix of how you see yourself and how your culture defines what a "girl" or a "boy" looks like and acts like. Cultures and communities of people today and throughout history have held different ideas about

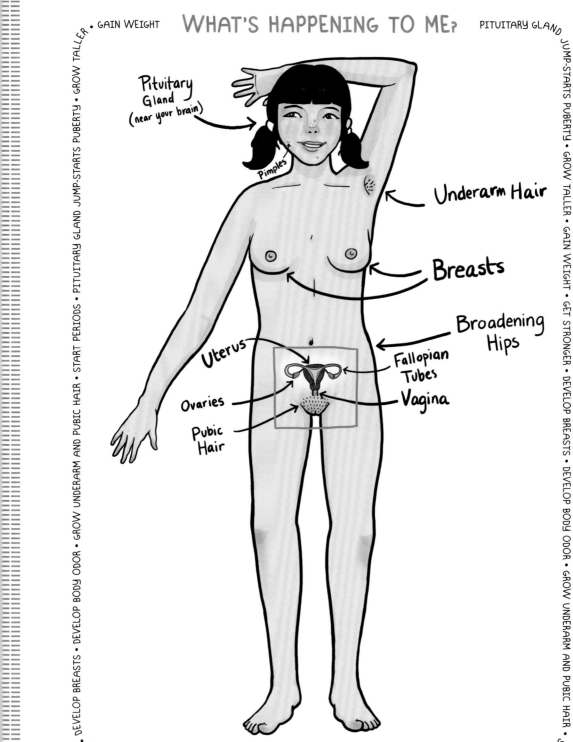

what they see as important for gender—what people wear, how they communicate, and whether they are teachers, leaders, or warriors.

Sometimes it can feel confusing when people expect girls to look and act a certain way that doesn't feel like *you*. Gender is just one part of who you are and it doesn't determine what you enjoy—whether it's playing baseball or working on an art project—or how you dress, act, or look. Your gender also doesn't determine who you fall in love with or who your friends are. It's possible that someone whose gender *identity* is a girl might have been born with some of the *biological* body parts or hormones of a boy. You *may* know a person as a girl because she wears a dress, or chooses to be called by a girl's name, or simply asks to be known as a girl. You *may not* know if they have different body parts or hormones. What is important is knowing each other as special, interesting, unique individual people and remembering that *all* people want to feel important, included, known, and loved.

In this book we are usually referring to someone's biological sex when we say "girl" or "boy," but we know that things are more complicated than that. We're usually talking about what most people experience when they go through puberty. Maybe your story will be different than most people's and that's OK too! Everyone needs to have information about their bodies to help them be *healthy and safe*. This book has information for *you* and for *all* kids. Keep reading!

. . . .

I am wondering how your body decides to be a BOY OR GIRL.

When a baby is born, body parts—like a penis and testes or a vagina and ovaries—help tell the biological sex of a baby. It is rare for a baby to be born with body parts of both male and female, but it could happen for lots of reasons. Sometimes it takes puberty for these kids to figure out what gender makes sense for them.

Most people with a vagina and uterus *feel* like they are girls and most people with a penis and testes *feel* like they are boys. And sometimes someone's body parts and how they see themselves doesn't match up—like when a person with boy body parts sees themselves as a girl or a person with girl body parts sees themselves as a boy—they may describe themselves as transgender. How we see ourselves is called our gender identity.

. . . .

What if you want to talk about stuff but you are TOO SHY?

Talking about puberty can sometimes feel awkward because you are mentioning body parts that are usually hidden, and seeing changes to your body that are new and sometimes unfamiliar. Plus, you don't hear people talking about it in everyday conversations at the dinner table or the bus stop: "Hey—your puberty is really looking great!" However, there are three guarantees about puberty that might make things easier. First, everyone grows up, so you are not alone. Second, lots of people are shy and uncertain about how to talk about puberty, so you are not alone on this either. Third, a lot of people—your parents, teachers, friends, brothers and sisters, and grandparents—want the whole puberty experience to go well for you and would love to help you out.

. . . .

What BODY PART does puberty start at?

The whole process of puberty starts in your brain in a small gland called the pituitary. The pituitary gland sends a message to your ovaries that signals your body to begin growing and changing. (Wonder where your ovaries are? Check out the picture on page 4 to see.) Your ovaries then send hormones (chemicals that travel around in your blood) to alert the rest of your body to start all of these changes. The primary hormone of puberty for girls is called estrogen, but progesterone and a small amount of testosterone also help out with all of the changes of puberty.

What will "GROWING UP" do to my future? Am I really ready to have all these changes in my life, at the age of ten?

"Growing up" is the work of becoming a grown-up. Your body and brain are changing to prepare you for doing all sorts of things in the future—like driving a car, having a baby, working at a job, buying groceries, being in love, reaching for the cookie jar . . . you get the idea! The word *puberty* describes how your *body* grows from a kid's body to a grown-up's body, and the word "adolescence" describes how your *brain* changes to make adult decisions and have adult relationships. Put together, growing up *takes many years*, so don't worry—you've got some time before you are officially grown-up!

. . . .

Will I still have puberty when I am FIFTY?

Puberty is officially over when your body stops growing. So most girls' bodies finish puberty when they're teenagers. However, our bodies continue to change in interesting ways *our whole lives*.

. . . .

How will going through puberty affect my soccer GAME?

Your new height and weight might make you *faster or slower* on the field; you might need bigger shoes and a bigger uniform; or you might need to pack a tampon or pad in your duffel bag (see Chapter 7 for more on that!). But you can still be a soccer superstar while you're going through puberty.

Is it important to have a DOOR to your ROOM during puberty?

When you are *going through puberty*, it can sometimes feel like your whole body is in a construction zone as it transforms into an adult shape and size. That can make you feel more self-conscious and make you want more **privacy**. Having a **place** where you can **think through** things on your own without interruptions can be helpful. As important as all of this is, it's not a requirement for someone in puberty to have their own door or even their own room. However, that doesn't mean that you can't *look for safe places* where you can be by yourself. You might find it helpful to keep a journal where you can write down your experiences and feelings.

What do you say when a FRIEND ASKS YOU A QUESTION about puberty and their mom hasn't told them anything about it? Do you answer?

When someone asks you a question it means they trust you for information, and they are hoping that you will answer without teasing them or making them feel stupid or silly. Acknowledging someone's curiosity and interest is the first place to start. Then give them a brief answer if you feel you know what to say. Finish with an idea of where they could find more information. Something like this: "That's a great question—*I had that same one*. When someone bumps into me or hugs me too tight *my breasts really hurt*, almost like a bruise. It has something to do with them growing. I have a book that is helpful. Want to borrow it?"

Does puberty make you TIRED?

How we *take care of our bodies* can impact how they grow during puberty. With so much happening, our bodies need the fuel from healthy food and good sleep in order to grow well. While your body is sleeping, chemicals in your brain and bloodstream that influence your growth are going to work—your body and your brain need sleep to do the work of growing. It is entirely typical for someone going through puberty to need about nine or ten hours of sleep each night. Many people going through puberty feel tired from all of that growing *plus* all of the things they do all day—like hanging with friends, riding bikes, and working on math problems!

When you are all "grown up," do you WISH you were a kid?

I know that some kids wish they were adults at times and some adults wish they were kids at times—but I think people are generally happiest when they like being who they are right then and there.

Will I change my ATTITUDE when I go through puberty and do something like smoke or get tattoos?

While our bodies are going through puberty, our brains are undergoing changes too. In fact, our brains continue to mature even after our bodies have finished puberty. Your body might be finished growing sometime in high school, but your brain will continue the work of wiring itself for making adult decisions into your early twenties. Making decisions about how to care for our bodies is part of growing up. There is no reason that you ever need to say yes to things that are dangerous to your health (like smoking) or permanent (like tattoos). *Waiting until your brain matures* and you can weigh the consequences of your choices is a great option.

. . . .

Why are there so many MEAN WORDS about a woman's body parts?

I know it sounds odd, but when people feel something is mysterious, sacred, or very important, they sometimes try to *diminish the idea* by giving it a mean name. I think they feel it shrinks the big idea down to a smaller idea that they are more comfortable with, and that they can laugh at instead of talk about. Using mean words for women's body parts happens when people don't know quite what to do with the mystery or importance of our bodies. And sometimes people use those words because they hear them being used by others, and they think that if they say the same things, they'll be more cool or interesting. Most commonly, you hear nicknames or mean words about the body parts that are uniquely female—like "boobs" or "tits" instead of "breasts." There are nicknames for boys' body parts too. People generally don't make up mean words about the body parts we all share. As people mature and see their own and each other's bodies as worthy of care and honor, their words change to reflect their understanding.

What I Am Most Looking Forward to in Puberty

- Becoming taller so I can reach things
- I am most excited for a new me
- What I am looking forward to is pretty bras
- I am looking forward to just start and not be worried about it anymore
- I am looking forward to the end
- I can't wait till I can date! Most of my friends aren't into that yet, but I am
- I have different feelings of growing older; it's a big responsibility, but I want to grow older because I want the responsibility
- I am looking forward to seeing how my body changes and if I will have zits or not
- Having breasts
- Getting stronger and more beautiful
- Knowing how it's all going to turn out

2. I'm Five Foot Three and Wear Size Nine Shoes. Does That Mean I'll Start **Puberty** Soon?

. . . And Other Questions About Growing Taller, Gaining Weight, and Changing Shape

How do you evolve the PERFECT BODY?

Each person's body is *perfect* in all its imperfections. Perhaps your ears are uneven, or you have a birthmark on your leg, or your nose is a little crooked. Sometimes when we see other people's bodies we wish our body looked similar—theirs may seem more "perfect" than yours. You might wish you were taller, bigger, rounder, straighter . . . when really your body is just right for *you*. Sometimes when our bodies are changing—like during puberty—we are especially self-conscious about how our bodies compare to others'.

In the moments when you are worried *most* about whether your body is *perfect* enough, try making a list of all the things you are grateful your body can do, like seeing, tasting, moving, or feeling. When you focus on *gratitude* you are reminded of all the ways your body is at work for you. Even when you're not thinking about it, your body is breathing, digesting, moving, and pumping blood through your heart. You may find that being grateful about your body changes the way you see it and honor it—you just might realize how *perfect* it is.

. . . .

What is the BEST kind of FOOD to eat when in puberty?

Eating **healthy food** gives your body what it needs to get *taller and stronger*. You need enough calories and fuel to think well, write poetry, study, and run plays on the basketball court. Calcium and protein fuel bone and muscle development, iron builds healthy blood cells, while fruits, vegetables, and grains give your body vitamins and minerals to stay healthy and give you **energy**.

In particular, girls in puberty need to get enough calcium in their diets to build strong bones. Puberty is a time when you develop most of your adult bones. When you are in puberty, your body absorbs **calcium** better than it does when you're an adult, so it's important to make certain you have enough calcium now in order to have healthy **bones** later. Calcium can be found in dairy products like yogurt, cheese, and milk; in dark green vegetables like broccoli and spinach; and in other foods like salmon. As you are building strong bones, it is helpful to surround them with strong muscles by including protein in your diet. And while you are getting stronger, add some iron-rich foods while you're at it, like green leafy vegetables and beans, to make your blood stronger too. Fueling our bodies is an important part of being healthy.

If my mom is five foot four inches tall and my dad is five foot eight inches tall and I am very small for my age and I am in the sixth grade, HOW TALL am I going to be?

How tall you become depends a lot on how tall other members of your birth family are—you will most likely be close to the height of the other people to whom you are genetically connected. A girl between the ages of eight and thirteen can grow anywhere from two to ten inches during puberty. But how tall will you be exactly? That's going to be a surprise. Did you know that most of your growing happens while you are sleeping? Sleep is important during puberty because it allows your brain and body to rest and rejuvenate from your busy day, *and* it provides important time for your body to grow. It would be typical for someone in puberty to need nine or ten hours of sleep a night.

. . . .

I'm five foot three inches tall and wear size nine shoes. Does that mean I'll start PUBERTY soon?

There isn't a certain height, weight, or shoe size that means you are officially starting puberty. However, a significant change in height and/or weight (called a growth spurt) and an increase in shoe size is one of the first signs that a girl is starting puberty. A growth spurt can look very different for different people, and *sometimes people don't even notice!* Perhaps one person grows an inch every year and then suddenly grows four inches taller in one year. Someone else might grow a quarter of an inch every year and now grows one whole inch over the same amount of time. Both girls grew four times more than they have ever grown in a single year. Two people, two different amounts of growth, and yet both are in a growth spurt and both *may be starting puberty.*

What if I have not GAINED WEIGHT or GROWN for a year?

Growing taller and *gaining weight* happens gradually—and not always as fast or as evenly as we would like. Sometimes someone grows a lot, then doesn't seem to grow as much for a while, and then grows really quickly again. It is also possible that you are growing, but it doesn't seem like it because your friends are growing more quickly right now. The definition of the end of puberty is when we stop growing—so it's possible that you are coming to the end of the puberty experience.

. . . .

I've gotten FAT this year. Will it go away?

Gaining weight is an essential part of puberty. If we grew taller without putting on any weight, then we'd eventually need special cement shoes to keep our feet on the ground during windstorms! Our bodies need to add weight and *healthy amounts of body fat* to work well and to grow the way they are meant to during puberty. Body fat stores vitamins that we need to stay healthy; protects some of our organs, like our livers and stomachs; is a major building block of our brains; and is a part of every body cell.

Girls between the ages of eight and thirteen might gain anywhere from fifteen to fifty-five pounds during puberty. And healthy girls during puberty add about twice as much fat to their bodies as healthy boys do—it's an expected and necessary part of their body's development. It is totally possible for someone to grow tall and *then* put on weight—and it is totally possible to put on weight and *then* get taller. Read on for more advice about gaining healthy weight during puberty.

. . . .

Why do your THIGHS get big?

As your hormones increase in puberty, your body gains weight. In fact, gaining weight is an important part of staying healthy in puberty. Your body shape also changes—hips and thighs broaden, and your breasts grow. It is typical for a girl to add fat to her body around her hips and thighs; this fat prepares her body for *a possible pregnancy* in the future. Women who are pregnant use the extra fat stores as energy and fuel throughout pregnancy and while they are nursing babies. In healthy-weight females, fat does not increase significantly after a woman is in her early twenties.

. . . .

At what age should a girl start to worry about LOSING WEIGHT?

Gaining weight is part of what you can expect in puberty (check out the question on page 15 on getting "fat") since your body is growing and changing shape, and you're storing more fat on your body. As an adult woman, your body needs to grow and develop in healthy ways, which means weighing the right amount to give your body the *fuel it needs to work well*. Sometimes in our culture, it can seem like women are always talking about losing weight—about being dissatisfied with the way their bodies look. Losing weight is for people who know that they weigh more than what is ideal for their health. In some cultures gaining weight and having your body get rounder is a sign of great beauty. *Asking your doctor or nurse* what weight is recommended for your height, activity level, size, and age will help you make wise choices.

. . . .

Can you talk a little bit about ANOREXIA?

Anorexia nervosa is a condition in which someone limits the amount of food they eat or increases the amount of exercise they do to lose weight *beyond what is healthy for their body*. Anorexia nervosa occurs when someone has the idea that their body is "fat" and that they need to lose an excessive amount of weight even if their body needs *more* weight to function well. People who experience anorexia nervosa require support and help from experts to understand how to keep their bodies at a healthy weight. It's important to *talk to a trusted adult* if you feel like you are overly concerned about losing weight or if you feel a friend is struggling with this problem.

3. How Many **Pimples** Do You Usually Get?

. . . And Other Questions About Zits and Acne

I am NOT looking forward to having pimples . . . what do I do to handle them?

Keeping your skin clean every day by washing it with a mild soap or cleanser can reduce the amount of germs and bacteria on it. Washing your skin also creates less opportunity for them to be trapped and create a pimple. But it will not prevent all pimples. Sometimes no matter what we do, pimples show up.

For the occasional pimple that everyone gets, the ingredients found to be most effective in pimple management are *benzoyl peroxide* and *salicylic acid*. You can find pimple-treating products with benzoyl peroxide or salicylic acid in a regular grocery store or in your neighborhood pharmacy. There are additional solutions that can be very effective in helping your skin clear up as well. *Getting advice from a physician* is a great next step if you need more information. The good news is that as we get older, our skin gets less oily over time and most people experience pimples less frequently.

HOW BIG do pimples get? (I hope not too big; it would be sort of embarrassing.)

Because pimples are **uninvited** interruptions to our otherwise dazzling good looks *and* appear on our faces, necks, chests, and backs, they can definitely be **annoying** and sometimes even **embarrassing**. You can be certain that almost every single human being knows what a pain a pimple can be, either because they have had one or because they will soon get one. Teasing someone about a pimple is only funny when yours is bigger. **Pimples** and other skin-related challenges like blackheads can be different sizes. The good news is, no matter how big pimples get, they *typically only last a few days* and there are ways of treating them when they show up.

. . . .

When will your pimples STOP GROWING? I've heard it can take ten years.

Our **skin** changes throughout our lives. You don't often see a two-year-old with a lot of pimples, and you don't often see a ninety-two-year-old with a lot of pimples. When our bodies are going through puberty the new **hormones** change some of the glands in our skin, causing them to produce more oil, and that oil can sometimes clog a pore with dead skin cells and bacteria. That then creates a small **infection**—or pimple. However, it is not uncommon for people to have *occasional* pimples throughout their adult lives as bacteria can get trapped even in less oily skin.

. . . .

How many pimples do you usually get?

Contrary to popular thinking, how many pimples you get does not have much to do with eating chocolate or pizza. There are many factors that contribute to how many pimples people experience—including things you *can't* control like your puberty hormones and the **skin type** you inherit from your birth parents, and things you *can* control like how you take **care** of your skin. You may find that there are *certain foods or stresses* you experience that make you more susceptible to a **breakout**, so you can certainly pay attention to those—and they may be the same or different than what causes pimples for your good friend.

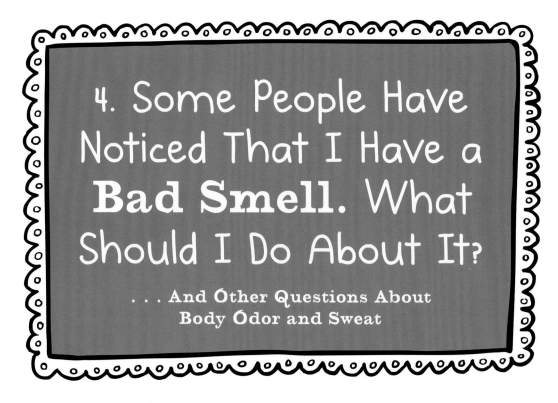

4. Some People Have Noticed That I Have a **Bad Smell.** What Should I Do About It?

. . . And Other Questions About Body Odor and Sweat

Some people have noticed that I have a BAD smell. What should I do about it?

Our bodies can create a lot of unpleasant smells—from sweaty underarms to farts to bad breath to stinky feet! Sometimes we don't even notice that we have all these smells because *our noses get used to our own bodies*. Usually if people are mentioning a "bad smell" now that you are in puberty, it probably means it's time to pay attention to keeping your body clean! If you are not interested in having a sweaty smell all day, then showering or rinsing off your body on a regular basis so that there is less sweat and fewer bacteria to combine with your sweat would

help. Places where sweat accumulates need special attention: under your arms, between your legs, and on the bottoms of your feet. Sometimes people wear deodorant or antiperspirant under their arms in addition to showering. Antiperspirants reduce the amount of sweat on the skin where you apply it—often under your arms. That way, the sweat and bacteria don't mix. Deodorants "deodorize" and change the smell of the sweat that has been broken down by bacteria. Deodorants allow your body to sweat. You can buy deodorants for foot odor as well. Since sweating is a useful thing, I *recommend a deodorant* if you are looking for something beyond a shower. Don't forget about brushing your teeth and keeping your hair clean too—it's part of the whole package!

When you are about nine you get SWEAT under your arms. At what age does it stop?

Your **whole body** has actually had the ability to sweat since you were born; it's *how your body naturally cools off* when you get too warm. You will continue to sweat your entire life. What you may have noticed is that when you are in puberty, your body actually sweats *more*—especially under your arms. Sweat, by itself, does not have any particular smell. Once you start puberty, though, hormonal changes alter the composition of your sweat; when the sweat comes in contact with the bacteria that live naturally on your skin, it creates a stronger odor. A sweaty two-year-old smells different than a sweaty twelve-year-old.

One of my friends has a lot of B.O. Should I tell them or not?

People's **perception** of body odor differs *across cultures and circumstances.* Body odor may seem perfectly fine in the locker room after basketball practice, but it may not be as pleasant at your family dinner table. Some people live in cultures where a sweaty smell is seen as a natural part of a hard day's work, while people in other cultures find it annoying and think it should be avoided. Most likely your friend will start to perceive her **body odor** with time. If you choose to bring it up with your friend, *you might include your own experience* so that your friend will be less embarrassed: "I have sure been smelling sweaty lately—but I have a new favorite deodorant. It smells like lemon and really works! You might like it too."

·····································

I have noticed that eating certain foods changes the way I smell. Is that possible?

Yes! Certain **foods** change the way our bodies smell in several different ways. Eating asparagus makes our urine smell different. **Strong-tasting** foods like garlic change our breath and sweat, and their smells can stay on our skin longer than other foods. Some foods create **gasses** in our digestive systems that come out as farts. Some people are more sensitive to certain foods and how their bodies process them, *so food can have different effects on different people.*

5. Why Do You Need a Bra in the First Place?

. . . And Other Questions About Breasts and Bras

I am in the fifth grade. Should I be wearing a bra? Why do you need a bra in the first place?

Although many of your friends and family members might wear a bra—many people in the world don't have access to bras, don't feel they need a bra, and don't even own one! There are **zero rules** about when someone has to wear a bra—in fifth grade *or any age*. There are all sorts of reasons people might choose to wear a bra. One reason is that bras **support** breasts. When running on the soccer field or jumping rope, girls often find wearing a bra *more comfortable*. Sometimes people wear one because they like the way they look or feel when they wear it. Sometimes girls wear a bra entirely because they think they are "supposed to" since all of their friends wear them, and they want to look the same as their friends. *Throughout your life* you might make different **choices** about when or if you wear a bra. What is important is that you think through *what seems right for you*.

My friends say I need a bra but I'm TOO EMBARRASSED to ask for one. What should I do?

Being embarrassed is a pretty **natural feeling**. It's not like you have had a lot of opportunities to ask for a bra before, and having breasts is also a new experience. No one needs to buy a bra because her friends say so. If you think it would be helpful to have a bra to support your breasts, or because it seems interesting or comfortable, or if you are just curious, sometimes asking a trusted adult is the most **challenging** part. This is probably because saying out loud that you would like to have a bra can feel like you are announcing to the world in a loud voice, "**I have breasts.**" Sometimes the easiest way to ask about something that is embarrassing is to *wait until you are alone with a trusted adult*—like a parent, aunt, grandparent, or teacher. Maybe when you are sitting together in a car or walking side by side, when you feel **ready**, you could say something like, "I was thinking it would be kind of interesting to look into getting a bra. Would you be able to help me with that?"

. . . .

How do I ask my parent for a padded bra because I really want one?

People wear **padded bras** when they would like their breasts to appear bigger or a different shape than they are naturally. When someone has had surgery on a breast or is wearing special clothes that need a certain fit, it can sometimes be helpful to have additional support or padding. You might want to **think through** what your reasons are *for wanting a padded bra*. Sometimes people think that a certain size or shape of breast is more beautiful or interesting, when beauty is never actually limited to a single body part.

My friend told me if you eat a lot of corn, you grow breasts faster. Is this true?

There aren't any specific foods that make breasts grow **faster**, or **bigger**, or differently. How fast our bodies grow and how large or small our breasts become have a lot to do with our birth parents and the size of their bodies and breasts. It also has something to do with how we **take care** of our bodies—with enough food, sleep, and exercise. *Every body is unique,* and the size and pace of puberty cannot be determined by a single food. However, our bodies need to have enough of the right foods to grow well overall (see page 13 for more on healthy eating).

. . . .

HOW LONG does it take for breasts to grow?

Your breasts start as small bumps underneath your nipples. You may have noticed small bumps—or you may have noticed that when someone runs into you in the hall or gives you a big hug, your nipples feel **tender**, almost like they are bruised. The bumps and the tenderness are evidence that breast tissue is developing. *It usually takes a couple of years* for breasts to **fully develop**. However, even when breasts are finished growing, they *continue to change their size and shape* throughout your life. It may seem to you like breasts are supposed to look a certain way, but there are as many different shapes and sizes of breasts as there are people in the world. Breasts of all sizes and shapes make it possible for a mother to feed her baby. In fact, it's pretty amazing to consider that all female mammals have this capability.

One of my breasts has been bigger than my other one for a while. Is this normal?

Because you have two breasts side by side, you might think that they would grow together at the exact same time in the exact same way. But in fact, breasts grow independently from each other. It's not unusual for one breast to start developing for a month or two before the other breast begins to grow. Even when they are finished growing, it would be completely typical for one breast to look bigger or be different in shape from the other breast.

. . . .

I have a cat that pushes down on my breasts— will it damage them?

Breasts are resilient to cats pushing down on them—also dogs, hamsters, and turtles! Sometimes when breasts are developing they can feel tender—almost like a bruise—when they are touched or bumped or pushed down on by cats. That feeling *is just breast tissue growing* and tends to go away in a couple of years when breasts have finished growing.

. . . .

What are the STRETCH MARKS for on your breasts?

Stretch marks happen on places of your body where your skin has experienced rapid growth or weight gain. The "marks" are where layers of skin can have different colors from the skin stretching. Not everyone gets stretch marks, and some people get them on places other than their breasts. Stretch marks will sometimes go away or become less visible over time. They do not change how breasts or other body parts work. *People of all ages and genders get stretch marks.*

6. Why Is **Pubic Hair** Curly When I Have Straight Hair?

. . . And Other Questions About Hair in New and Interesting Places

When is the average age of someone who SHAVES THEIR LEGS?

Across cultures and throughout history there have been different ideas and practices for removing body hair—sometimes those ideas are different for women and men. For lots of women there are cultural ideas around removing hair from their legs, underarms, pubic area, and eyebrows.

There are all sorts of reasons someone might choose to remove body hair—beauty, sports, religion, tradition, comfort, because their friends and family do. And there are all sorts of reasons that someone would never remove body hair—beauty, sports, religion, tradition, comfort, and because their friends and family *don't*. I bet if we asked all the women around the world at what age they began shaving their legs, there would be so many women who don't shave their legs that the *average age* would be "never." You might find that when you ask *your* friends or people in *your* family, you get a different answer. That's probably because in the place you live people choose to remove their body hair. In the end, it's a personal choice.

My grandma told me that once I shave my legs, I need to shave my legs the REST OF MY LIFE. Is that true?

Sometimes people think if you shave your legs, the hair on your legs will change forever—that you will have more hair and that it will be darker and more coarse. When you use a razor to shave hair and it begins to grow back, the hair sometimes seems darker and feels prickly. But actually shaving or waxing your hair does not change the color or the hair itself—it just appears that way when it first grows back. This is because shaving cuts each individual hair shaft off at a sharp edge, so when it first grows back, *it's not as soft*. But if you were to let the hair grow out again, with time the hair would eventually appear like it did before you started shaving. Hair darkens on most people as they get older *but not because they shave* their hair.

· ·

I am questioning the hair. DOES IT HURT when it grows?

Hair doesn't hurt as it grows. *Your hair doesn't have any nerves* (the threads connected to our brains that communicate pain), which is why it doesn't hurt when you cut hair either.

· ·

Can you wake up one day and have a lot of PUBIC HAIR?

It is possible that one day you'll be in the shower and you'll become suddenly aware that you have pubic hair you never noticed before. Sometimes that is because *we are not always paying attention*—especially during everyday events like taking a shower—to all the different parts of our bodies. Pubic hair can be difficult to spot when it first starts growing, since it starts slowly and its color can blend into the hair that's already on your body. Pubic hair often becomes coarser in texture and darker as we get older.

. . . .

What is the point of PUBIC HAIR?

What an intriguing question! It hardly seems like humans need pubic hair to stay warm or to make us more interesting looking, since most of the time it is hidden from view. Most likely, pubic hair is left over from *millions of years ago*, before people had clothes and they needed more hair covering their whole bodies to keep them warm. Pubic hair can be helpful in protecting our bodies from dirt, bacteria, or abrasion.

. . . .

When you have ARMPIT HAIR is it OK if you cut it with scissors or is it better to shave it?

Cutting your underarm hair with scissors would definitely be tricky! There are a number of safer ways to remove hair from under your arms or other places if you decide it is important to you. Most people who are interested in removing their hair use a razor on wet, lubricated skin (using shaving cream or soap as a lubricant helps the razor glide on the skin more easily and reduces the possibility of irritation). Other people choose to wax their hair. This involves applying a warm liquid wax and then pulling the wax off quickly—much like removing a bandage. (I recommend having an expert help you with this if you think it sounds interesting to try.) *Removing body hair* can sometimes create irritated skin or cause a hair to grow back at an angle into the skin (this is called an "ingrown hair"), creating an infection that is easily treatable but sometimes annoying.

How much hair do you get in your ARMPITS if you don't shave? (In inches.)

The *thickness, color, and length* of your hair usually follows patterns established by family genetics—the messages we receive about our bodies from our birth parents and their parents. However, most underarm hair does not get longer than *a couple of inches* even if you don't cut or shave it.

Why is pubic hair curly when I have straight hair?

Wild, isn't it? Because pubic hair and underarm hair are a part of our puberty experience, they are the result of our **hormones** changing. Hormones also seem to sometimes affect hair follicles—the areas in the skin where hair grows. The hair **follicles** in your underarms and between your legs are actually a different shape than the hair follicles on your head where your straight hair grows. These differently shaped follicles can create *curly hairs*.

. . . .

What should I do about pubic hair if I swim?

If you are asking what to do if you think others can see your pubic hair when you wear your **swimsuit** and that doesn't feel comfortable to you, there are ways to remove hair through shaving or waxing. However, sometimes removing body hair creates irritation of your skin and it would also reduce the protection of pubic hair. It's important to remember that pubic hair is a **human experience**—one that happens to all people around the world. Keeping in mind that someone who notices your pubic hair would be seeing something that also happens to them might help you feel less self-conscious.

. . . .

Does puberty make all of your hair curly, even on your head?

It is quite **common** that our hormones will **change** the curliness of all of our hair—*not just pubic and underarm hair*. Sometimes people in puberty will go from straight or wavy hair on their heads to very curly hair, or from curly hair to straight or wavy hair!

7. What If I Have My **Period** for the First Time at School?

. . . And Other Questions About Periods

So what is a PERIOD exactly?

The last *new* thing that happens to most girls' bodies during puberty is the beginning of their period. As your body grows and develops on the outside, it grows and changes on the inside as well. (To understand these internal changes, it helps to have a picture of all the body parts involved—turn to page 37 and take a look.) You have a uterus that is found inside your body just below your belly button and above your pubic bone. Your uterus is about the size of your fist—so a baby girl's uterus is much smaller than an adult's uterus. The uterus is where the baby grows while a woman is pregnant—so just picture how big it can get! Attached to the uterus are two fallopian tubes and connected to those tubes are ovaries. (An ovary in an adult woman is about the size of a large olive.) Inside your two ovaries are *millions of eggs*—microscopic cells that have been there since you were born. Now that you are in puberty, hormones signal an egg to be released one at a time from an ovary. The egg travels into the fallopian tube and then into the uterus. While the tiny egg is traveling, a cup or so of fluid is collecting in the uterus, getting ready for the egg's arrival. Since this egg is traveling alone and not meeting up with a sperm (more on sperm and eggs meeting up

TAMPONS

32

in Chapter 13), the egg and the fluid leave your body through your vagina. The fluid, which contains a tablespoon or two of blood, and the tiny egg that leave your body are called a **period**. The entire process from the egg being released to its leaving your body is called **menstruation** or the *menstrual cycle*.

. . . .

Why is it called MENstruation? Why MEN?

That's an excellent question! The official word for a period is **menstruation**, but many people call the experience a **period**. And since most men don't menstruate, maybe we need to rename it *womenstruation*! The word menstruation actually comes from the word **menses**, which means "month"—and women typically have periods monthly.

. . . .

Can you predict when your first period will be?

Although it's *impossible to predict the exact day* your first period will appear, your body provides some **clues** that can tell you the general time that your body is preparing to have your first period. First, your body needs to be close to its adult **size** to begin having a period. Sometimes the leanest girls—either tall or short— are the last to start their periods because their bodies haven't gotten close enough to an adult weight yet. Second, most girls have pubic hair before they have their first period. Third, many girls notice a small amount of fluid—a white sticky substance in their underwear—that shows up occasionally and may occur months before their period. This is nothing to worry about—it's just fluid from your vagina that shows you that your body is **getting ready** for a period. You will have that same fluid before your first period and before every period throughout your period life. And finally, the **average** age for a girl in the United States to start her period is about twelve years old. "Average" means that there are girls who are starting their periods at age nine or earlier and girls who are starting at age fourteen or later.

Does your period last forever?

Periods last for a **period** of your life. You start your period during puberty and you stop having periods when you're about fifty years old.

. . . .

Did you say that your period lasts four to seven days or forty-seven days?

The time of fluid leaving our bodies *typically lasts four to seven days and nights*, although some women have periods that last a few days **more** or **less**.

. . . .

I'm only eleven and I have my period. I'm the only one in my class and I'm really embarrassed. WHAT SHOULD I DO?

Eleven is a very **typical age** to start having a period. And, unless you have asked all the girls in your class, you may not be the only one who has started. You really can't tell from looking at someone whether they have had their period or not. Being **self-conscious** and shy about having your period is not unusual—*it's a new experience*, and you need to get used to everything involved with it. I am confident that even if you are the first, it won't be long until others are also having periods. Sometimes it's helpful to recognize that being first is like being a **pioneer**—soon, others might be looking to you for ideas since you will be the one *with the most experience*!

What do you do if you've been waiting, waiting, waiting, and YOUR PERIOD doesn't happen?

The entire experience of puberty takes several years—periods start a couple of years after you notice your breasts beginning to develop. When all of your friends have gone through puberty faster than you have, it can feel like it takes forever. Sometimes it can be especially challenging because everyone is talking about something you haven't experienced yet. Remember, your experience will be *uniquely your own*. However, if you feel like you are still waiting for some of the signs that your period will start and you are fourteen years old or older, it is helpful to talk to a doctor or nurse to check in and get more information.

. . . .

What is it like when you first get your period? What is your first feeling?

When a period starts—whether it is your first period or your two hundredth period—you may first notice a small amount of warm wetness between your legs. Sometimes it is difficult to tell that your period has started until you go to the bathroom to check. You will be able to tell because period fluid is reddish in color, from the small amount of blood present, so you will see it on your underwear and possibly on your pants or other clothing. Your first period may look very dark red or brown in color.

. . . .

Do you start out with pads, tampons, or what?

Because your period is red, it will show up on your clothes if you don't protect them. Today, there are several options to take care of this. Two popular choices are pads and tampons. Many people like to start with pads because they are the simplest to figure out. Keep reading!

Why do women wear the pads on their vagina?

Made of cottony material, pads are worn *inside your underwear* on the *outside of your body* during a period. There are all different sizes of pads—long, short, thin, or thick. *Some even have wings*! They catch the period fluid by absorbing it after it leaves your vagina. You wear the pad during the days and nights you have a period. You change your pad throughout the day as needed. On a typical period day, you might change a pad five to ten times. Most pads attach to your underwear with an adhesive strip, so it is very easy to put on and take off and stays in place even on a busy and active day. Some pads are disposable, so when you are ready to change it, you throw it in the garbage wrapped in a small amount of toilet paper. Some pads are made from cloth so that they are reusable once you have washed and dried them. *Pads have changed a lot throughout history*. Ask someone a generation or two older what pads were like when they were your age and you'll be surprised at the answer!

. . . .

Can I wear a tampon?

Like pads, tampons absorb the fluid of your period—but instead of being on the outside of your body like a pad, a tampon goes inside your vagina to *absorb the fluid before it leaves your body*. Putting in a tampon takes motivation and a bit of practice, but anyone can try it. Some girls wait to try a tampon until they are older or have had some time getting used to the other logistics of a period. Some people never wear a tampon. It's possible to try a tampon the very *first* minute of your very *first* period.

Tampons come in *several sizes*, and not all tampons have applicators. If you are thinking about trying a tampon, it's helpful to start with the smallest-sized tampon and one with an applicator. Applicators are made of cardboard or plastic—some girls find the plastic applicators to be an easier place to start. It can be interesting and helpful to look at a tampon before you try to put it in—open up the package and take one apart to see how it all works together.

Fallopian Tube
Where eggs travel

Uterus
Where periods start
and babies grow

Ovary
Where eggs
are stored

Cervix
Opening to
the uterus

Vagina

Opening to
the vagina

Clitoris

Urethra

Vaginal
Opening

Labia

Anus

How do you stick a tampon in your vagina?

When you are ready to try a tampon, first use the toilet if you need to so that you can **relax** all the muscles you typically use to hold back urine. While continuing to sit on the toilet, open up any packaging or paper surrounding the tampon applicator. You will see ridges in the center where you put your thumb and middle finger. Your index finger rests on the end where the string comes out. Using your other hand, open the lips of your labia and place the tip of the applicator (the opposite end from the string) up against your vagina. (A picture of how this all looks helps a lot! Check out page 37 to see these body parts up close.) The key idea here is to **insert** the tip of the applicator at an **angle** that points toward your backbone. Your vagina is actually tilted at an angle to your back. After inserting the applicator tip, you can begin to push the plunger on the applicator with your index finger while holding the ridges in the center of the applicator so that the tampon will *slide into your vagina.* When your index finger has pushed the end up to the ridges, you can pull the applicator out, leaving the tampon in—with the string outside of your body. *You did it*! The string will be helpful in removing the tampon. Keep reading!

. . . .

What if I have tried putting a tampon in and it doesn't work?

Don't worry if it doesn't feel *like a smooth process* the first time, or even if it doesn't work out—it often takes a few times to get used to the **logistics**. A girl also has a thin membrane covering the opening of her vagina called a **hymen** that can sometimes make trying a tampon more **challenging**. Your hymen can be stretched or torn from day-to-day activities like riding a bike or having period fluid come out. But if your hymen has not been stretched or broken, the tampon might meet **resistance**. If you don't have success on the first attempt, you can always try later. In the meantime, pads are a great alternative. It can be helpful if you have an adult or someone older to talk you through the process. There are also instructions in the boxes of tampons for additional information and help.

What if I accidentally put the tampon in the wrong hole? Or in too far?

It can be helpful to be familiar with how your body looks between your legs so that you can find your vagina more easily. Using a mirror and spending a minute finding your vagina will *make things a bit easier*. As a girl, you have three openings between your legs: your urethra, where urine (pee) leaves your bladder; your vagina, which leads to your uterus; and your anus, where undigested waste (poop) leaves your body. You do not need to worry about accidentally putting a tampon in your urethra—*it is far too small*. And if you accidentally put a tampon in your anus, you would recognize you were in the wrong spot by how it feels.

It is impossible to put a tampon in too far—you do not need to worry about it getting lost and floating around in your body so that it comes out of your ear in social studies class! Your cervix will keep a tampon from going any further than where it belongs. (Check out the picture on page 37 to see all these body parts!)

. . . .

Tampons kind of scare me. Pushing something inside my body, could I hurt myself?

One of the easiest mistakes to make as you are practicing and learning how to put a tampon in is to not get it in far enough. The muscles surrounding your vagina are strong, so when a tampon is inserted only part of the way, the muscles surrounding the tampon will tighten around it and make standing up without pain difficult. If this happens, the thing to do is to remove the tampon and start over with a new one.

The good news about wearing a tampon is that when it is in correctly, *you cannot feel it*. The bad news about wearing a tampon correctly is that you cannot feel it. That means it's *possible* to forget you have a tampon in! When someone wears the same tampon for too long because they forgot about it, bacteria can grow and make them sick—this is called *toxic shock syndrome*. Wearing a tampon requires remembering to take it out and replacing it with another tampon or a pad during the four to seven days and nights of your period. You will know it is time to change your tampon when you can sense that it is no longer being helpful in absorbing fluid.

A great idea is to change your tampon every time you go to the bathroom, or *about every four hours*. Remove your tampon by pulling on the string gently, remembering to keep those muscles relaxed—*it will slide right out*. Wrap up the tampon in toilet paper and throw it in the garbage. Some women only wear a tampon when they would find it more helpful than a pad—like when they are swimming or playing sports—and they wear a pad other times of the day and night.

. . . .

The thing I am most worried about is will people know just by looking at me that I had my period?

If your clothes are protected with a pad, a tampon, or even a "pad" you have made from toilet paper, no one will be able to tell from looking at you. Taking a shower every day when you are having a period keeps your body clean and removes any of the period fluid that can create an odor over time. By *taking care of yourself and your body* during your period, you'll be sure that no one will be able to tell unless you bring it up. Wild as it is to think about, you are probably around people all the time who are having their periods—in the grocery store, at school, coaching volleyball, or on the chess team. They're all around you, and you have never noticed they were having a period.

No one is required to know if you are having your period, but if it feels helpful to you to let someone know in order to get support or help, *speak up*! Typically there is someone in a school office responsible for the students' health—like a nurse—who has pads and other supplies and is prepared to help you. Also in the office there is often backup clothing and a chance to call someone if you need to. Camp counselors, piano teachers, soccer coaches, and chess club advisors will *all* be understanding if you need to bring them in to help you navigate the *logistics of a period*.

What if I have my period for the first time at school? And what if I have my period during a piano lesson in the middle of a really long Bach piece?!

There are two *guaranteed* things about a period: first, the exact moment it starts will be a surprise; and second, there are all sorts of people who can help problem-solve with you and want it to go well for you. Being caught off guard by your period requires creativity and ingenuity—and creative and ingenious is just what you are!

Whether you are in math class or at a piano lesson, when your period starts, it can be very distracting, but it is *not an emergency*. Asking the teacher to be excused for a minute to go to the restroom is a good first step. If your period has started and you are worried that people will notice period fluid on the back of your clothes while you're walking to the bathroom, you can wrap something like a sweatshirt around your waist, or pull your shirt out to cover your pants or skirt. If you forgot your sweatshirt, you can hold something like a book or a backpack behind you as you exit. If you are somewhere where you don't have a tampon or a pad, you can make a temporary pad out of toilet paper. Generally, *unless you draw attention to this moment*, people are not looking for periods on each other.

. . . .

Is it uncomfortable to have a period at night?

It is no more uncomfortable to have a period at night than during the day. You don't need to worry about setting an alarm clock to wake up every four hours to change a tampon at night—just wear a pad instead.

. . . .

What do you do if you get your period while you're swimming? Freaked out!

Swimming while having a period requires some thought and planning. Let's talk it through so that you will feel prepared. There are a couple of *challenges to consider*. First, if you are wearing just a swimsuit and your period starts, it will be more apparent than if you were wearing a pair of jeans or shorts, because the red fluid of your period won't have a second layer of clothing to keep it contained. Second, if you wear a pad to protect your swimsuit, it is easy to see the pad because it is on the outside of your body. And third, a pad can't distinguish between period fluid and pool water, so a pad won't really absorb period fluid if you are swimming with it on.

What can you do? Remember, period fluid only comes out in small amounts at a time. So if you have your period and you want to jump in the ocean to cool off on a hot day or swim in a relay at the swim meet, taking off your pad and being in the water for a short amount of time is not a problem. You will want to put a pad back on, and maybe a pair of shorts or a swim cover-up, if you sit on the beach to hang out or build a sand castle. Many times girls who are swimmers or who spend a lot of time at the beach find that wearing a tampon works best since tampons *absorb the fluid inside of your vagina.*

. . . .

The first time a period happens, do most girls feel uncomfortable or scared?

There are girls all over the world who have never had an opportunity to talk to someone about periods before their own show up. I can imagine that seeing reddish-brownish fluid in my underwear would be frightening if I had not had anyone tell me that it might happen. I can also imagine that there are girls who feel nervous about getting their periods *even when* they know everything there is to know about periods. But there are also girls who look forward to getting their periods because they want to be part of something important. Periods show us that our bodies are becoming adult and that they are developing in a healthy way.

. . . .

How can I tell someone if I started my period?

Talking to people about your period can seem awkward or scary because it is something brand new and seems kind of unusual. Sometimes we're not even sure how we feel about it ourselves. *Remember,* some grown-ups have never had practice talking about periods either—perhaps they never talked to their parents about them. That means they feel just as shy or uncertain about the conversation as you do. Your mom, or another trusted adult, might have some helpful ideas on how you can manage your period throughout your day. There are all sorts of people in your life that want this to go well for you—dads, moms, grandparents, cousins, siblings, teachers, coaches, camp counselors, and friends. Remembering that can be helpful. Then, *find a moment* when you are alone together—maybe while you're walking the dog or riding in the car can be a good time to start a conversation: "I want you to know that my period started."

DOES IT HURT? Why do some girls feel icky when they have their period? I hear some girls throw up!

If you put one hundred women in a room and ask them if having their periods "hurts" or "feels icky," some of the women would say "yes, absolutely," some would say "not really," and the rest would say "sometimes yes and sometimes no." Not everyone who has a period feels "icky" or throws up or has a painful experience. However, *some do*. It is also common to experience discomfort during some periods and not during others.

Some of the experiences that "feel icky" might include having a headache, lower backache, upset stomach, sensitive breasts, or cramps in your uterus. Often these feelings are more apparent in the first couple days of a period and improve toward the end of a period. Taking care of your body and treating the pain or discomfort is important. *Staying active, exercising, and stretching* are often the most helpful ways to relieve some of these feelings. Some people find that putting something warm on their lower backs or lower bellies helps.

It is a *good idea to ask for help* if you find that how you feel during your periods is keeping you from the activities that you usually enjoy. A doctor or nurse practitioner often has helpful solutions for your specific needs.

Your grandmothers and great-grandmothers were probably cautioned not to play sports or dance when they had their periods. They were often also told not to go to the dentist or have their hair curled, or even washed, while menstruating. Today we know it is important for girls to stay active, eat and drink healthy foods, and get adequate sleep during their periods—the *best ways* to care for their bodies.

What I Am Least Looking Forward to in Puberty

- People not liking me because I look different or I like different things
- I am least looking forward to the middle of puberty
- I am worried about how people will react when I get a bra
- Thing I am most worried about is how do I get my tampon in
- What I will look like and if I will be able to pass all my grades
- The hair in unusual places
- Your period will happen until you're fifty, and that's a very long time
- Getting zits; both of my parents had thousands of zits
- I am worried about having arm hairs and friends seeing them
- Sweating
- If I have my period out of my house

What do you think might happen when a CAVE WOMAN had their period?

Because there isn't much information about the daily lives of cave women, we can only imagine some of the ways they managed their periods. One way might have been that they wore *animal skins* or used *plants* to help absorb their periods. It might even have been that nobody noticed or cared. Or they might have had a special place that women gathered during their periods where they would stay together while they were menstruating.

It's interesting to think of women across history and the challenges they may have faced. I often think about women today, and throughout time, who have walked long distances over many days or months while menstruating—like traveling the Oregon Trail as pioneers, or crossing a desert in a caravan. Those women have *managed their periods* without being able to run to the grocery store to get supplies. There are girls who live in places even today who do not have access to pads and tampons. They would have different choices to make about managing their periods than you do.

. . . .

Is it true you STOP GROWING when you start your period?

The very last *new* thing that happens to you during puberty is starting your period. But puberty doesn't officially end until you stop growing. Typically, when a girl's period starts she still has some growing to do—maybe a couple of inches, but probably not ten! By the time your period starts, the *majority of your growing* has occurred.

Why is chocolate such a big asset to having a period, as a helpful thing?

Sometimes you hear women talk about how a few days before their periods they crave certain foods. Researchers have tried to find out if women want certain foods for a reason, but they still have more questions than answers. What we *do* know is that how we take care of our bodies during our periods is important—we need to continue to eat a diet that includes calcium, fruits, vegetables, grains, iron, and protein. Sadly, it is not recommended for girls to *only* eat chocolate!

. . . .

How do you make your period MORE FUN?

Many girls can't imagine drawing attention to starting their periods. However, in *some cultures around the world*, a girl's first period, or finishing puberty, is celebrated—it's a time of honor as a girl's body becomes like an adult's. In Japan, some girls eat a special meal of red beans when they get their first period to signify "good fortune." In South Africa, some communities have a tradition of giving girls a beautiful red beaded bracelet to mark the occasion. In parts of India, some girls are honored at parties that include traditional foods, saris, and jewelry. In parts of Eastern Asia, girls who have started their periods live in white huts, wear white clothes, and eat white foods for a whole year. In Jewish culture, some girls study to have bat mitzvahs, where they assume the new responsibilities of adulthood in their communities. In the Latino community, a girl might celebrate becoming an adult at a quinceañera where her family and friends honor and toast her. In the Apache culture, there is a tradition of singing and dancing to affirm a girl's life. My neighbor and her mother chose to mark the occasion of her first period with a special dinner together in a favorite restaurant. Perhaps celebrating with a parent or friend would be a way to honor this transition—sounds like a lot of fun!

If you have a period at a certain time does it CHANGE YOU?

Having a period will change some of the day-to-day things you do during the four to seven days of menstruation. However, it does not have to change the person that you are *or the person that you are becoming.* Remember, there are women who have competed in the Olympics and won gold medals while having a period. There are women who have written beautiful poetry and prize-winning literature while having a period. There are women who have campaigned for social justice, lived in jungles and deserts, fought in combat, and traveled in space shuttles, all while having a period. Although it can feel a bit overwhelming at the beginning—and even a little scary as you hear about it for the first time—women all over the world and throughout history have managed periods while they do other important work.

8. How **Moody** Can You Get?

... And Other Questions About Feelings and Emotions

How moody can you get?

Sometimes people say **teenagers** are "moody"—or have a lot of **moods**—because it's easy to tell what a teenager is feeling by what they are doing or saying. Teenagers express their moods more often than adults. The **emotion** center of a teenager's brain is very active. This is partially because the hormones responsible for puberty add to the excitement our brains feel when we have emotions—almost like *turning up the volume on a radio*. But it also has to do with the way our brains develop. Between the time of puberty and our early twenties, our brains build connections for how to manage our feelings when we make decisions. While our bodies are under construction, our **brains** are under construction too!

. . . .

How should I deal with my feelings if I feel a zillion things at once and don't know who to tell or what?

When you feel **overwhelmed** by your emotions, a good place to start is to give your feelings a name. If you find your face red, your stomach upset, and your voice loud, perhaps you could label your emotion "mad," "frustrated," or "discouraged." When you feel quiet, kind of shaky, and unable to talk without tears in your eyes, perhaps you can call that emotion "sad," "disappointed," or "embarrassed." *By labeling our emotions and feelings*, we help our brains define them, and when we define our **emotions**, we get better at finding specific **solutions** to manage them. Sometimes *writing in a journal* can be helpful since it gives you a place to describe how your body feels and the situation that made it feel that way. By writing these things down, you may be able to have a better understanding of why you feel the way you do, and when you have a better understanding, solutions may become clearer. Many people find that talking with a **trusted** person is helpful. For some kids that might be a parent, family member, or older sibling. For others, that might be a counselor or other expert.

. . . .

Do you still have mood swings when you are older?

Yes! All people have **moods** that change throughout a day or an event. Since adults' brains have had more experiences and time to be wired, grown-ups probably won't act on their feelings in the same way or as often as teens and kids. So even though adults have **many emotions** throughout a day, you might not be able to tell by how they look and act.

. . . .

Do mood swings always make you GRUMPY? Thanks!

A **mood swing** is when your mood quickly changes from one mood to another. It could mean you are happy one minute and then sad the next. It could mean that you are grumpy in the morning at breakfast, but then you are laughing loudly at lunch. Sometimes people talk about mood swings only when someone's mood is negative, but mood swings happen *any time our moods change*. Having different feelings throughout the day is a natural part of the way our brains work and it tells us and others how we are responding to what is happening around us. *Learning how to manage and communicate our emotions* in healthy ways is one of the most important parts of growing up.

. . . .

Why do I CRY when I do not know why?

Crying has been a helpful part of your **communication** your whole life. When you were little and didn't have the language skills you have now, it was one of the only ways you could communicate fear, hunger, or a wet diaper. *Even as we get older*, sometimes crying offers a physical **relief** that helps manage or communicate our feelings. People cry when they feel all sorts of emotions—sad, scared, lonely, angry, happy, confused, frustrated, unheard, anxious, unloved, without hope, or surprised. Some people cry easily, and some people have a hard time crying out loud.

. . . .

I wish someone knew how sad I am all the time. What should I do?

Everyone feels sad **some of the time**. It's **normal** to feel sad when you are worried about something or someone; you feel disappointed, discouraged, or lonely; or you have experienced a loss. You should let someone know if your sadness interferes with your ability to do the things you love or makes it hard to think about anything else. **Talking to someone** can help you feel less alone, and they might even be able to make you feel better. If you feel sad a *lot* of the time or most of the time, it's *important* to talk to a trusted adult—like a parent, teacher, or counselor—to stay *healthy and safe*.

I have been getting mad really easily at home and with my friends. Does that have anything to do with puberty?

Getting mad is a **normal** part of the human experience—it can communicate disappointment, discouragement, embarrassment, or something else. Sometimes if your emotional response is *big*, it's helpful to remember to **take a break** for a moment and give your body a chance to get **calm**. Taking deep breaths, listening to some music, or getting some exercise are all helpful options. It is almost impossible to come up with good solutions to challenges when we feel super angry. However, it's also important to *pay attention* to situations where you find yourself mad because it might give you **insight** into something that is important to you.

. . . .

How can you control your emotions if you don't have a lot of time?

We can pay attention to our emotions by **watching** and **listening** to our bodies' responses. We can get information about how our body reacts AND what calms our emotions. This brings us the focus and attention that allow us to problem-solve. When we practice being **attentive** to our feelings in lots of different situations, we can figure out how to calm our bodies more easily and effortlessly. And being calm helps us become better decision makers.

Why do I feel SO self-conscious?!

Going through puberty is like having your body and your brain under construction. There are many changes to get used to, like learning how to take care of your skin and managing your period, more sweat, and new hair. *That is a lot of work!* In addition, you are experiencing new emotions and situations that you need to work through, and that takes a lot of thought as well. Most people in puberty feel like they are the center of attention and they worry that *everyone* in the room is noticing their pimple or that they have B.O. or that they are embarrassed. The good news for you is that when everyone is only thinking about **themselves**, perhaps they will be so busy worrying that *you* are going to notice *their* pimple that they might not see yours!

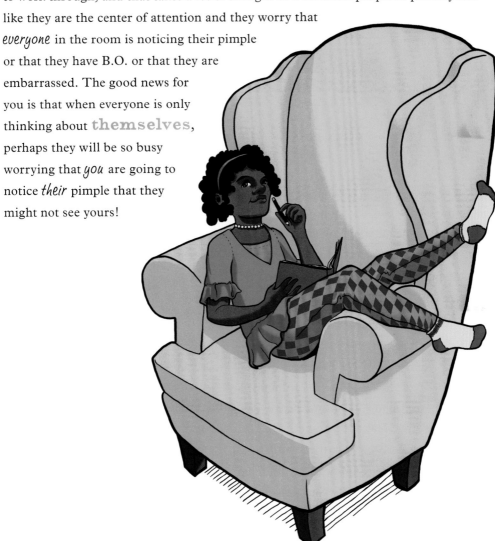

9. Do Girls in Puberty **Gossip?**

. . . And Other Questions About Friendships

What if a person you don't like is BEING TEASED, and you don't really want to stand up for them but you don't like seeing people get teased?

I haven't met a single person who hasn't experienced either being teased or watching someone else get teased. People often tease others when they feel afraid of something themselves. For instance, if a person teases someone, she is trying to point out someone else's problem so that others don't point out her own concern. *We know two facts about teasing*. The first is that no one really looks forward to being teased, especially when it is unkind. The second thing we know is that if you hear someone being teased and you simply speak up or help redirect the subject, instead of adding to the laughter or the teasing, often the teasing will stop. That's because if the teaser doesn't get a response, then they don't have an audience for their "joke." Talking to a grown-up can sometimes be helpful if you need someone to discuss your ideas with. Sometimes it can be a grown-up who *does* the teasing and they don't understand that their words are hurtful. Adults occasionally use teasing and sarcasm to try to be funny. In that case, it might be helpful to talk to another trusted adult who can help you *communicate your feelings*.

Do girls in puberty gossip?

Yes, sometimes they do. Gossiping means sharing information about someone with others when the person you are talking about is not there. Gossiping often includes sharing stories that are not your business to talk about—and sometimes may not even be true. Gossiping can be tempting because it points out another person's problem instead of yours. You can feel like you're part of the group when you join in on the gossip, but the problem is that the group is defined by *gossiping* instead of by something more meaningful. What makes gossiping unhealthy is that the person you are talking about does not have the opportunity to share their own version of the story. *Sadly, there is no age limit to gossiping,* and almost everyone does it—even a little bit—at some point. Somehow talking about other people negatively can make us feel more important, but it *doesn't help us be a good friend.*

Why would someone want to be popular by being mean?

When people are mean, sometimes it's because they are trying to feel important or more powerful by making other people feel bad. Sometimes they do it because deep down, they feel afraid or uncertain, so they *cover up their feelings* by acting big and powerful. The definition of being popular is when someone is well liked by many people. Sometimes people mix up being powerful with being popular, because powerful people *demand a lot of attention*. People give it to them because they are afraid or worried about what will happen if they don't. It is rare that people are truly popular *and* mean—most likely people who are mean are powerful, but they are not actually popular. Truly popular people are the ones who are admired by others because they help them feel important and included.

. . . .

If two girls are always whispering and acting like you're interrupting their private joke, what should you do? HOW DOES ONE COPE?

Whispering is a lot like gossiping because you are sharing information without letting others in on the conversation. It is a way for people to feel like they're important because they have *something to say*. Healthy conversations among friends include laughter, debate, sharing your feelings, and honesty. You may need to *take a break* from these friends who whisper until they *choose a different way* to bring others into their conversation. I am certain you are not alone in your challenges with kids whispering—I can imagine you would find others who would be interested in joining you in another activity.

What I Wish My Friends Understood About Me:

- I want to be independent but still have a best friend
- I may act tough, like I don't care, but I do
- I really want to fit in more than anything
- I don't always want to fit in even though there is pressure to
- Sometimes I'm slow to share my ideas
- I can be very hard on myself sometimes
- I can be happy, but look sad, or be mad, but look happy
- I am really funny, although no one knows
- I have some issues with anxiety
- I never have the strength to speak up
- I sometimes feel like a bully who doesn't want to be one
- I am loyal
- I'm scared of lots of things
- I am strong
- I get angry easily
- I'm insecure about my popularity
- I like being different
- I know I talk a lot, and I know I am a leader, but sometimes I am lonely

What if you are in a fight with a friend and she thinks she's being nice and you are being mean, but you think the opposite?

Being a friend can be hard work. It can mean doing something that isn't your first choice but is what your friend wants to do. It can mean asking your friend to for-give you, or sticking up for her when it isn't easy to do. It is inevitable that there are also times when friends do not get along. In this case, maybe you need to find out what you *do* agree on in this argument to find some common ground.

. . . .

Can you tell us about PEER PRESSURE?

Sometimes peer pressure is when you believe your friends or other kids want you to do something that you *otherwise would not choose to do.* Sometimes you hear them say their ideas out loud ("Come on! Don't be a chicken, just jump!") and sometimes they don't say anything out loud but you believe they want you to do something ("They are going to think I am a chicken if I don't jump"). Peer pressure can also encourage you to try things you have never tried before. Someone might say, "Come on, don't be a chicken, join the chess club—we are all doing it!"

What is important is that you make your own decisions in partnership with your family's support and input. It's hard when you feel like you are the *only one* not participating and that you will lose the friendship of others if you choose not to join in what they are doing. Sometimes you will find that if you choose something other than what the group is suggesting, others will be relieved and join you.

My best friend is a boy. We're starting middle school next year and I've heard that sometimes people tease you if your best friend is a boy. What do I do?

Having a good friend is a wonderful thing. But being teased is not easy to manage, no matter what the circumstance. Sometimes, in middle school, people think a boy who is a friend must be a boyfriend—someone you have a crush on. Since we can't really control what others say or do, it's helpful to have some ideas of what *you* might do if that happens. First, you can **ignore** the comment. Sometimes when you don't give someone any response, they stop. Second, you can think of a funny line that will show you are **comfortable** with your friendship and what they think doesn't bother you. Or third, you can ask them to **stop** teasing or bring in another friend or adult to help you. Often, creating a scene by yelling, crying, or retaliating adds fuel to the fire and keeps the teasing going.

. . . .

I have a best friend that is a boy, but I want a best friend that is a girl, but I can't seem to have a friend that likes me at all.

Finding a friend that likes you often starts with **being a friend** to someone first. *That can be kind of scary*—especially if you are uncertain whether the person will like you at all. Being a friend means spending time together and **sharing** experiences. A fun place to start looking for a friend is while you're doing *something that you like to do*—you will find someone who also enjoys that same thing. If you like to sing, maybe you could find someone in music class or in a choir who wants to sing after school. Or if you like chess, maybe you could join the chess club to find someone who likes it as well. **Friends** often discover they have similar interests, and their friendship develops from time spent together doing those things. There will almost always be times in your life where finding friends is **challenging**—changing schools, moving, or having a friend move away are all times when you will need to have patience as you meet new people.

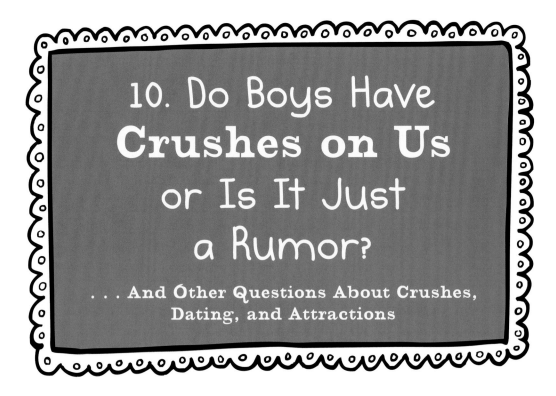

10. Do Boys Have **Crushes on Us** or Is It Just a Rumor?

. . . And Other Questions About Crushes, Dating, and Attractions

How does your body react when you have a crush?

When you have a **crush**, sometimes your body and mind feel more *alert and excited*—especially when you're thinking about your crush or in the same space as them. Your face might get red, your hands might feel sweaty, your stomach might do backflips, and your heart might beat faster. This is your body reacting to the experience of being **attracted to someone**. Our bodies respond to crushes similarly to other exciting or nerve-wracking experiences, like riding a roller coaster or giving an important speech. In these situations our brain chemistry changes to help our bodies prepare for the moment.

I have a CRUSH, and a BIG one! Is this OK, and how can I deal?

A crush usually means you are interested in someone in a bigger way than you are with other friends. Maybe you notice them more than you notice other people, and you'd like to be closer or spend more time with them. Having stronger feelings for people is a *natural part of growing up*. If you find that thinking about your crush is keeping you from talking to or being with other friends, then the crush is getting in the way. Finding safe places to get to know your crush, like at school or in a club, is a great way to build your friendship. When a relationship moves from a crush to a trusted friendship, and when you are ready and it feels safe, you can share your feelings with the person. But if you have an idea that the other person would not understand or that you are not ready, it is also OK to let the *exciting feelings* of liking someone stay private and not act on them.

Why do we have crushes when we're eleven but not six? When should you begin to "like" someone? Confused!

Sometimes it seems like *all of a sudden*, liking someone is all anyone can talk about. You may not have the same feelings because you have other things on your mind—that can be confusing! As you get older, you may find your feelings changing *from confused to interested*. It is pretty common when people are in puberty to start feeling attracted to each other in new ways, but it actually doesn't happen in a single moment—*it occurs over time*. And there is no specific age when those feelings should start. You may find that liking someone means also having sexual feelings for them, which is entirely normal—another human experience.

Do boys have crushes on us or is it just a rumor?

Almost everyone has **attractions** to people. Liking someone, caring about someone, appreciating someone—these are all terrific things that humans get to experience with each other. Sometimes these feelings lead to **relationships** or **friendships**, but they certainly don't have to. Your feelings are yours. And it's likely that as you grow up, you will like *lots* of people, and lots of people will like you, because there are lots of likable people! Girls can have crushes too—you might find another girl or boy crush-worthy. Sometimes you will enjoy liking someone, and sometimes it might not feel so comfortable. Part of growing up is learning how to be in **healthy** relationships.

. . . .

What is the right grade to start dating?

Dating is one of the experiences *couples choose* so that they can spend time together to **explore** their relationship. There are all sorts of "dates"—watching a movie, eating at a restaurant, going on a bike ride, or even just hanging out. Sometimes dating means just two people alone, and sometimes it means you are in a crowd or with a group. The whole idea of a date is to **get to know** each other better. Some families and cultures have a specific age in mind when they think dating is "right," or they think that it shouldn't happen at all, because they see it as a step toward a more serious relationship, and they want to make certain you are **safe** and **prepared**. You may have a different idea of what a "date" means than your family does. So a good way to look for answers would be to have a **conversation** with your family *where everyone can share their ideas*. As difficult as it is to see at times—especially when there are different ideas—parents are invested and interested in knowing who you are with, where you are going, and what your plans are so they can help you to be safe and have fun.

What I Wish Boys Understood About Girls:

- Laughing at girls does not make you cool
- We like it when you pass us Frisbees at recess
- We can't always be who you want us to be
- Sometimes girls act completely different around you than they do around other girls
- We do care
- Sometimes you aren't funny
- We like to be known by our personality rather than just our looks
- We don't have to be pretty to be a good girlfriend
- We do not like to be called "hot"
- We want to be friends with you
- We like to be talked to first
- We are not all the same; treat us as individuals
- The popular and powerful girls are not always the best company
- Girls have pressure to look and act a certain way
- It hurts to be teased

What is "gay"?

Being gay means being primarily attracted to other people of the **same gender** for romantic and sexual partnerships. People who are straight are primarily attracted to people of the opposite gender. Throughout history there have always been people who are **attracted** to the same gender and others who are attracted to the opposite gender or either gender. As you are growing up and exploring relationships and attractions, you will experience many feelings *for a wide range of people. Time and experiences* in all sorts of friendships and relationships help you **discover** and **understand** your sexuality.

11. How Can I Make **My Family** Seem Like More of an Option to Talk To?

. . . And Other Questions About Your Relationship with Your Parents

What if you like a boy but you don't know how to break it to your parents that their baby girl LIKES SOMEONE?

Talking with grown-ups about friendships and relationships can sometimes be challenging for a lot of reasons. They might be surprised by what you have to say, might change their opinions about you or your friend, or might have advice that you weren't looking for. "Liking" someone means you have feelings for the person that seem different than feelings you have for other friends—that you are interested in that person in a new or bigger way than you used to be. You may worry that your mom might not think you are old enough to *like* someone, and that she will be concerned or surprised. It can help to start off the conversation with something like, "Some of my feelings are changing about people. I think I like someone in my class and *I would like to tell you about it* but I am worried what you will say or think."

It seems like my mom and I are FIGHTING ALL THE TIME. I just think she doesn't understand. She thinks I don't understand. It's, well, it's majorly weird! What do I do?

Living with your family gives you an important place to learn skills that you'll use *throughout the rest of your life*. However, it isn't always easy for parents and kids to get along. Sometimes there are topics or emotions that are uncomfortable and difficult. Maybe you feel like your mom gives you too much advice or that her ideas don't feel realistic. Maybe you think she is critical, or you argue more than anything else. It might be helpful to just *talk about talking* with your mom. Try to find a time to connect when there isn't something to argue about. You could start with, "It always seems like we are arguing—it would be nice to talk things over without yelling at each other." Let her know how you are feeling—*most likely she is hoping for some changes as well*. If you find you are always fighting, learning how to take a break and come back together when you both calm down can be key. Families who are struggling may need to call upon resources like counselors to help them work on ways to improve their communication.

. . . .

How can I make MY FAMILY seem like more of an option to talk to?

Sometimes it's challenging to bring up certain topics with your family. That might be because they don't have any practice talking about those topics, which makes them feel as uncomfortable as you do. Maybe you feel like they don't "hear" what you are trying to say. Or maybe just finding a time to talk is half the challenge—grown-ups can be distracted by lots of responsibilities, so you need to invite them into the conversation. You might try saying something like, "*I would love to talk through something* that is going on with my friends. Would

What I Wish Parents Understood:

- How hard it is to repeat myself when I didn't want to tell you in the first place
- You do not need to re-vacuum the living room after I do
- Sometimes we want to talk to you
- Yelling does not make me listen
- It is hard having to worry about everything
- I don't want to say how my day went after it was super tiring
- I don't like it when they compliment everything; I want real input on what I do
- That I will make the "right" decisions when hanging out with my friends or guys
- How sad I am, and how much I'm going through
- That when we are moody we don't mean to be mean or angry
- I have weird clothes that are too little kid-ish
- That most of us are very responsible and are able to take care of ourselves, and we all stress at least a little bit about the way we look
- We want your help but sometimes (a lot of times) we want to do things on our own too

you have some time after dinner?" Or, "Would you want to walk the dog together tonight? *I have something on my mind*." Sometimes it's easier to start the conversation by writing them a note.

. . . .

My family doesn't like to see me growing up, so I don't know how they will accept that I am growing up. How can I show them kindly that I'm NOT A BABY anymore?

Sometimes our bodies and our brains *change so fast* that our parents can't keep track. And sometimes we feel ready to have new responsibilities, but our parents are less certain. Every family makes adjustments as each person grows up, and part of the process is *negotiating decisions within a family*. If you feel ready to make your own decision but your family is less certain, have a conversation with them to say what you are thinking and experiencing. Everyone has the courage for even a one-minute conversation—it's a place to start.

. . . .

Should my dad know I am going through puberty?

Dads are invested in their daughters' lives in puberty *and beyond*! Some dads may not have much experience talking about girls' body changes since they have only been through their own puberty experience. Using your own words and stories will *help your dad understand* what puberty is like for a girl. Dads can be amazing advocates—they want the puberty experience to go well for their daughters. Sharing your *thoughts and feelings* with your dad helps him to discover some of the ways you are growing up.

Why do teens start to HATE their parents?

Becoming a teenager does not mean you will automatically hate your parents. In fact, most teens say that their parents are the *most important people in their lives*. As we get older, we begin to develop our own ideas and opinions, and sometimes those ideas are different from our parents' ideas, which creates conflict. As we work through our conflicts with our families, it's important to take a break from the conversation when it gets too heated, coming back to it when we can be calmer. It's also important to look for things that we can agree on and to make compromises when we can't agree. *Living with your family helps you* to learn about how to get along with others, how to love others, how to be challenged, and how to grow.

. . . .

Why do I think that sometimes MY FAMILY is driving me crazy?

Have you ever noticed that your family members can be your biggest cheerleaders and *at the same time* they are the people that bug you the most? That's because families are where some of our most important growing up takes place. We learn about ourselves while living with our families because we practice how to be in relationships, get along, have major arguments, and share space, responsibilities, and time. Everyone in the family is learning how to live together and navigate through *life* . . . it's not easy.

In every healthy family some of the decisions are made by the grown-ups, some by the kids, while other decisions are *shared*. When you are little, most of the decisions are made by the grown-ups; then, as you get older, more and more of the decisions are shared; and *finally, with practice*, more and more of the decisions become your own. Sometimes as we are growing up we believe that we are ready to make our own decisions before the grown-ups do. This can be frustrating *and* annoying for everyone because everyone sees the world differently. It can help to talk about how your family determines when someone is old enough to take part in making their own decisions.

12. Why Do Boys Grunt Instead of Talk?

. . . And Other Questions Girls Have About Boys and Their Bodies

 ## Do girls have totally different FEELINGS than boys?

Emotions communicate to others and yourself how you respond to an experience. Boys have the **same emotions** as girls—sad, mad, happy, jealous, disappointed, etc. Sometimes we have a certain idea that boys are supposed to act and feel one way and girls another, so we are surprised when we see something different. But *the same experience* may draw out a completely **different** response in one person than it does in another. It can seem like boys feel less sad or scared—maybe a boy tells a joke or laughs at a sad moment in a movie or responds in some other way that doesn't seem to match your own feelings at the time. However, it is important to recognize that *boys have feelings too*. Sometimes in our **culture** boys aren't given the same **permission** to show and share their emotions as girls. *Can you imagine how hard that would be?*

. . . .

Do boys feel as awkward as girls do about puberty?

Boys **worry** over a lot of the same things that girls do about puberty. Will someone notice I have pimples? Am I the right size? Am I **normal?** Will the person I like like me back? Because puberty is a *human experience*, everyone has some of the **same concerns**.

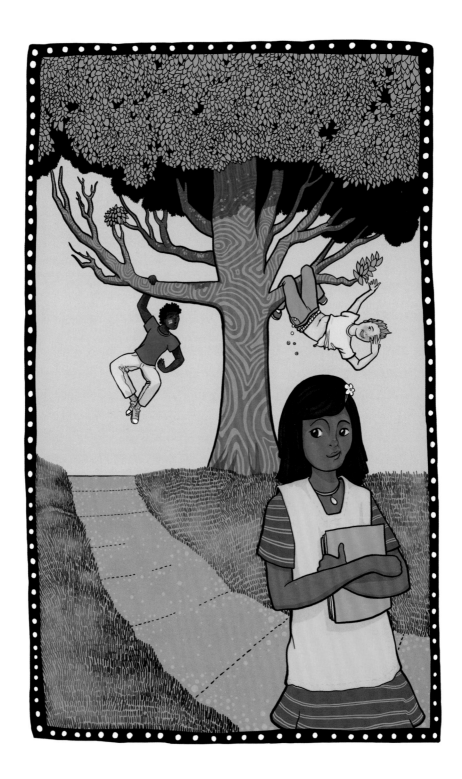

Why do boys grunt instead of talk?

Boys have a lot of important things to say. There are talkative people and quieter people, and sometimes it might seem like boys use fewer words than girls to express themselves, but that is *certainly not always the case*. When someone uses fewer words it may mean they are shy or unsure about what to say or they don't feel adding more words is necessary. Sometimes talkative people use their words to process their experience. What is important for talkative people to remember is to *leave space* in the conversation by pausing, so others can add their ideas. And it's helpful for quieter people to remember that their words are important to contribute.

. . . .

Why do boys have bigger ARM MUSCLES? It's not fair!

Both boys and girls develop stronger and bigger muscles as they go through puberty. However, you are right, boys will typically get broader shoulders and bigger arms than girls. Testosterone is the primary hormone that changes a boy's body during puberty. And even though girls also have a small amount of testosterone (in addition to their primary hormones called estrogen and progesterone) the *significant testosterone level in boys* helps to create larger and more defined muscles. Everyone can continue to develop their muscles throughout their lifetime through exercise and weight training.

. . . .

My question is why do penises GO UP? Why can't they just stay down?

A girl's body typically has *three* openings between her legs: a urethra that connects to the bladder, a vagina that leads to the uterus, and an anus that is at the end of the intestines and the digestive system. All three openings have their own unique functions. A boy's body typically has *two* openings: a urethra in the penis that is shared between his bladder and his testicles, and an anus that connects to his digestive system. So a penis has two jobs to do. Its regular job is being available to **pee**, and its new job that starts during puberty is to **release sperm**. To do its new job, a penis changes its shape in order to keep the urethra from getting mixed up in its work! In order to release sperm, a penis will change from *relaxed to straight and erect*. After the work of releasing sperm, it goes back to relaxed so that it can be available to release urine. (Is it hard to picture all of this? Check out the illustrations on page 40 on the boys' side to put it all together.)

. . . .

When a penis goes up does it SHOOT UP or does it slowly lift up?

A penis gets **erect** when *blood fills up the vessels in it*. An erection can happen when a penis is touched or when a boy has sexual feelings or thoughts—or sometimes, especially when a boy is in puberty, it can happen just because! Erections happen when a boy is expecting it to go erect, or when it is inconvenient, like while a boy is giving a speech in front of the class. A penis usually goes erect over **seconds**, not minutes.

. . . .

Does the penis get STIFF just overnight? When it does get stiff, does it hurt?

A penis can **become erect** (or stiff) during the **day** and during the **night**. *It does not hurt for the penis to be erect.* (More interesting facts about penises can be found in Chapter 8 on the boys' side.)

So at what age can a penis have an erection? Age eight? Age two? Age thirty-nine? What age?

A penis is able to go erect *even before a baby is born*. Because a penis is sensitive, especially to touch, it might go erect when a baby gets his diaper changed. However, it is not until **puberty** that sperm is available in the testicles to be released.

. . . .

Why do penises hurt when you step on them?

Throughout our bodies we have networks of **nerves** that alert our brains to pain or touch or tickling. In boys' and girls' bodies, many nerve cells surround the outside parts of our **reproductive organs**—like a penis and testicles or a clitoris (a small and particularly sensitive spot just above the urethra and vagina). These areas are very **sensitive** to touch and to pain.

. . . .

When boys have SPERM is it like how girls have a period and they have to wear pads and tampons? Can they control their "period thing"?

Boys' bodies do not have periods like girls' bodies. A girl releases a single egg one at a time and has a period over a few days, while a boy releases hundreds of millions of sperm in a **single moment**—more like a sneeze than a period. These many millions of sperm are released from the tip of the penis in about a teaspoon of white, cloudy fluid called **semen**. When a boy releases sperm, it is called **ejaculation**. Girls have a period about once a month *no matter what they think or do*, and boys can **release** sperm any time on any day. Since a penis generally needs to be touched to release semen, it rarely happens as a big surprise in the middle of math class, so boys do not wear anything to protect their clothing like girls do.

Do sperms have brains?

No, sperm do not have brains. *And penises don't know how* to make decisions on their own either. Only the person with the penis and the sperm has a brain.

. . . .

Where does sperm go during the day?

Millions and millions of sperm **hang out** during the day and the night in the testicles where they are produced until the moment they are released, which is called ejaculation.

. . . .

If you are Joe's best friend, and you know that he is having an ERECTION, and he doesn't know, should you tell him or not?

Joe knows. A boy can **feel** when he has an erection without even looking down to see if he does or not.

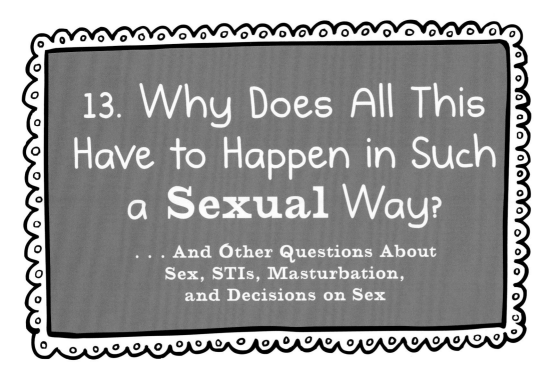

13. Why Does All This Have to Happen in Such a **Sexual** Way?

. . . And Other Questions About Sex, STIs, Masturbation, and Decisions on Sex

Do people have to plan or do something special to bring eggs and sperm together?

An egg inside an ovary can't just wake up one day and decide to become a baby. *Two people need to make a decision together* to bring their bodies so close that an erect penis can go inside a vagina. The penis then releases *hundreds of millions* of sperm in the vagina. Those millions of sperm swim through the cervix into the uterus and even up into the fallopian tubes. When there is an egg present, it takes only one tiny microscopic sperm to fertilize the egg—a single sperm actually enters the egg and then the egg shuts down to all the other sperm, becoming a brand-new cell. The brand-new cell is called a zygote. Then, the zygote starts to divide and divide and divide into more and more cells. The dividing group of cells travels down the fallopian tubes and plants itself on the lining of the uterus, where it continues to divide and grow. Eventually, it becomes a baby. Wild, isn't it? All of us started off as a *single tiny microscopic cell*!

How do the boys' and the girls' parts fit so perfectly together? Is it planned that way?

It is pretty **amazing** to think about . . . and kind of mysterious and sometimes challenging to picture. You are not the first person to shake their head at the whole idea! When two people bring their bodies so close together that an erect penis fits inside a vagina, we call that **sexual intercourse**. Some people shorten the words to **having sex,** and some people honor the action by saying words like **making love**. Whichever words you use, sexual intercourse involves two people making a decision *together* to bring their bodies *together* when the egg and sperm can come *together*. It's a lot of together! When two people of the same gender are sexual with each other we also call it "having sex" or "making love." All people have the capacity to show and share their love with their bodies, their feelings, and their words.

....

Can gay people have sex?

Yes. "Having sex" has **many definitions**. One is when a penis enters a vagina. But having sex also means when two people bring their **bodies** together in a **sexual** way. When two people of the same sex bring their bodies together to *show and share their love physically*, that is also called **having sex**.

....

How do people in wheelchairs have sex?

Whether or not the **mechanics** are the same, people in wheelchairs can *show and share their love* in many of the **same ways** that people who are not in wheelchairs do. They find a safe and private place to touch, kiss, and talk to their partners.

When do you know when you are READY to have sex?

Being "ready" generally means that both individuals that are thinking about having sexual intercourse are also thinking through what having sex will mean to them, both as individuals and as a couple. *Having sex*—bringing two bodies so **close** together that they actually fit together—is one of the biggest actions possible for human beings. Some people and families believe sexual intercourse belongs only in committed adult relationships where both people have the **maturity** to be ready.

. . . .

What is, in your opinion, the healthiest time to start a dating/sexual relationship?

A healthy sexual and dating relationship is when both people have an **equal voice** in sharing what is important to them. Feeling *heard* and *understood* is an important part of keeping a relationship safe. There is no particular age or time when people are ready to date or have sex. Some people make their decisions based on the guidelines set by their family or their faith background. Sometimes two people are friends first and then decide together to start dating.

. . . .

Do people have sex regularly?

Choosing to have sex is dependent on many things—feeling ready to act on your sexual feelings, having someone who also wants to have sex with you at that time, and being **together** with that person *in a safe place*. Some people never have sex, some have sex a few times in their lives, and some people have sex often.

What is masturbation about then?

Masturbation is when someone **touches** their own body parts to create a sexual response. There are people who **masturbate** and people who do not—kids and grown-ups—all over the world. It is a **choice** whether someone masturbates, and they generally choose to *because it feels good*. Sometimes people worry that masturbating will make them less healthy or make them act funny, but scientists and doctors have never found any truth to these worries. Masturbation can be a **safe** and **normal** choice when it's done in **private** and in balance with all the other activities in someone's life—like playing sports and doing homework! (There is more information about masturbation on the boys' side of the book on page 44.)

. . . .

Is masturbation good for you?

Throughout history *lots* of people have had *lots* of opinions about **masturbation**. Some have worried that when you touch your penis or your clitoris or other sexual body parts it will change or hurt you. Others think **touching** your own body to create sexual excitement and orgasm gives you more information about your body and how to **experience** *sexual pleasure* without risking pregnancy or disease. Having sexual feelings and thoughts is a normal part of growing up as your body changes and you have more experiences in relationships and attractions with other people.

Around what age do most people START having sex for life?

There is *no exact age* for people to start having sex for life. Being "ready" can mean that you feel **emotionally prepared** to be sexual with someone. Being ready can mean that you are *physically ready* to have sex. Being ready can mean that you are equipped to manage and understand the potential CONSEQUENCES of having sex, like a pregnancy or a sexually transmitted infection (STI). Being ready can mean being married or in a committed relationship. Being ready can mean being an adult. Being ready often means all of the above. And sometimes people have sex and then don't for a while.

Where is the most likely place to have sex?

Most people choose a **private** and **comfortable** place to have sex where both people can concentrate on each other and not be interrupted.

. . . .

Is it nice to have sex? Is it uncomfortable or comfortable?

People choose to have sex because it can be a **feel-good** experience both *physically and emotionally*. However, it's possible to have moments where it is less comfortable. Perhaps you are not in a comfortable location, perhaps you are **uncomfortable** about your feelings, or perhaps you are in an uncomfortable position with your bodies. When people who **love and respect** each other are uncomfortable in any way they should feel safe to talk it over and stop or make adjustments.

. . . .

Can two humans do sex ANY time? Or is it a time in the year the penis comes up?

Unlike some animals that have mating seasons, where the males and females have intercourse at a particular time of the year, there is *no special season* for two people to have sexual intercourse. A penis can come up (be erect) **any time** of the day or night, and two people can **decide** together to have sexual intercourse at any time of the year.

How long does it take to have sex? Can you have sex for longer?

The act of **sexual intercourse**—when it is a penis going inside a vagina—usually takes minutes, not hours or days. However, being **close** to someone and *showing and sharing your love* in anticipation of being sexual with someone can add to that total time.

. . . .

Does having sex hurt? On a scale of one to ten, what number?

Having sex means bringing two bodies *very close together*. It is possible—just like when we hug someone or shake hands—that, either intentionally or unintentionally, we might hurt someone. People generally **choose** to have sex because it brings **pleasure** to both people and it communicates **love** and commitment. If it hurts for any reason, then the person that feels pain can speak up to ask for something to change or stop. Earlier, we talked about how our bodies have nerves that communicate to our brains about touch or pain or tickling. There are lots of places on our bodies that have *an abundance of nerves*, so that when touched, they feel especially nice. Penises and testicles and vaginas and clitorises are places that have an abundance of nerves that make them very **sensitive** to touch. When people respect and care for each other while having sex, it can feel very good. When a penis releases sperm, it is called ejaculation, and it creates a sensation all over the body, called an orgasm, that is very **satisfying**. *Girls have orgasms too*, when their whole bodies are excited sexually and the muscles in their vaginas and uteruses contract. **It feels good**, but it has nothing to do with releasing an egg.

Do you HAVE to do sex?

Sexual activity is always your **choice**. It takes both people saying **yes**—two yeses—to make an agreement to be sexual together. When someone says yes to having sex, they can **always change their mind** at any time. As your body changes and you begin to have *sexual thoughts and feelings*, you can choose when or if you will act on those feelings. When two people are sexually active, they need to **talk and listen** to each other. Always be sure the other person understands and feels comfortable with the plan.

. . . .

Is it OK to be SCARED to have sex?

Treating the decision with **respect** and honoring your **feelings** is important when deciding to have sex. It is not unusual to be nervous or scared to have sex—it can be a sign that you are aware of the potential risks and consequences. When both people see themselves as ready to make the decision to have sex, when they feel they are in a **relationship** of love and respect and commitment, they may feel less scared. Some people wait until they are more grown up and can manage the relationship and the **consequences** of having sex. Because sex is one of the biggest human actions, it should be no surprise that you can have some of the biggest human consequences as a result of having sex. What are some of these? Well, *having a baby* is an amazingly huge consequence. And another big consequence can be sharing a *sexually transmitted infection*. We are going to have more conversations about both— just keep reading!

How can I do "it" without getting embarrassed? How do I ask someone to do "it"? It = sex.

When two people are in a relationship, they make all sorts of decisions together—like what movie they want to see, or whether to arrive early to the basketball game or leave at halftime. Decisions between two people require understanding, negotiation, listening, and talking. The same communication is needed between two people when they are making decisions about sex. It's helpful to pay attention to your feelings as you make decisions. Sometimes being embarrassed is a sign that you are not yet comfortable with your decision. There are *millions and millions* of things two people can do together before they even think about having sex—holding hands, walking the dog, kissing, going to the park, having dinner together, talking on the phone, debating, arguing, and laughing are just a few. *Most relationships* don't end up including having sex. Asking someone to do "it" typically means a relationship has had time to experience many other decisions and events so that sex feels like a natural progression—not a surprise question and not a choice made under pressure.

. . . .

Why can't someone grow sperm and an egg so they don't have to have sex?

Part of what makes us interesting and different from one another is that we have messages from *two different birth parents* that get brought together when an egg and sperm meet. Our sizes, hair colors, and even parts of our personalities are determined by heredity. If we each just had one birth parent contributing both cells, we would all be clones from generation to generation. Besides, families also *become more interesting* as we bring two different ones together when a baby is born.

Why does everyone think sexual intercourse is so gross except the people who are doing it?

Although our brains *are wired to be sexual* from the time we are born, it takes having **experiences** in **relationships** to help us understand how to interpret sexual feelings and make decisions about sex. People who wait to have sex until they have the **information** they need and the right person and relationship to share the experience with are more likely to enjoy having sex.

. . . .

Why do people have sex? It's so gross!

It's easy to think that having sex is gross *since it is hard to picture*. Sex involves body parts that you normally don't show others and feelings you have yet to experience. As your body and brain mature, you'll **learn** more about sex and have more sexual **feelings**. Those feelings and experiences will help you to have a better understanding of sex.

. . . .

That's weird how sex works. Do you have to do it?

No one ever has to have sex. *It is always your choice.* In fact, it is illegal to talk to someone about sexual ideas or touch someone sexually without their permission. It is important to speak to a trusted adult if you think someone has been bothering someone sexually without giving their **consent**. Sometimes when someone has been assaulted, they feel like it was their fault or they feel embarrassed, shy, ashamed, or afraid, which makes it hard to talk to someone about it. It is *so important* to speak up and get help from a trusted adult. There are many experts who have ways to provide **support**.

Does kISSING have anything to do with sex?

Many people kiss while having sex, but two people can **kiss** without ever having sex, and it is possible to have sex without kissing.

. . . .

Why, when people have sex, do they say they do more than what you told us about? Is it true that they do more?

Having sex is often described as bringing two **bodies** together so that a penis enters a vagina. However sex really doesn't require a penis *or* a vagina. You can **feel** sexual without having sex, and two people can *be* sexual just by a simple touch. People of the same or opposite genders can bring their bodies together sexually. "Having sex" can mean a variety of ways of being sexual between people and often-times includes kissing, touching, and holding each other.

. . . .

When people have sex, why do they breathe funny?

Just like *exercise*, the action of bringing two bodies together while having sex takes **energy**. It can also be very **exciting**, which can change someone's breathing so that it sounds deeper or more rapid. While people are having sex, their hearts will also beat faster, they might sweat from exertion, their muscles will contract, and their brains will experience pleasure—all of those experiences together is called an orgasm.

Does every penis fit in the vagina they want it to fit in?

Remember, a penis doesn't get to make any decisions on its own—it requires the person attached to the penis along with the person attached to the vagina to make a decision about sex. But most penises and vaginas fit together well.

. . . .

When you have sex, do you have to wait for the penis to be erected, or does it do it on command?

A penis needs to be erect to be firm enough to enter a vagina. No one can tell a penis to become erect. Generally, a penis will go erect with touch or with the *idea of it being touched*.

. . . .

Do you know when you are having sexual intercourse?

The action of *bringing bodies together* so that a penis enters a vagina is noticeable. Your two bodies are so close that you are skin to skin, and you can feel the penis go inside, so *you will know when it happens*. Both people get to be a part of the decision to have sexual intercourse.

Why does all this have to happen in such a SEXUAL WAY?

Being sexual is *part of being a* human being. Along with being sexual, we are also compassionate, curious, invested, competitive, emotional, and resilient. Sexuality is woven through who we are and is *wired into our brains*.

. . . .

I just want to know, do people talk about having sex and then go get undressed and do it?

Usually making the decision to have sex means *more than* just talking, undressing, and doing. Some people also like to have a romantic dinner before sex, listen to music, or hold and kiss each other in addition to having sex. Part of a sexual experience with someone can also mean *spending time together* in other ways in a safe and comfortable place.

. . . .

To have sex, do you have to say, "Hey, want to have sex tonight?" and plan it?

Having sex requires lots of talking and listening and paying attention to yourself and to your partner. It is important to *check in with each other* before, during, and after you are sexually active. Whether it involves a simple kiss or touch or something more, both people need to agree—that means *two yeses*. You can be confident about consent if you talk with your partner about what you have in mind. Then you can be sure that you both agree or you can change the plan together. Sometimes people are nervous or shy when talking about sex and this could lead to confusion or a misunderstanding. Talking and planning through the important questions like when, where, what, and how sex is going to happen builds trust and respect among partners.

Who thought of having sexual intercourse in the first place and how did they think of that?

Great question! From the beginning of **life on earth**, many plants and most animals have **reproduced** by fertilizing seeds and cells *to ensure their survival*. Since our *brains are wired* to be sexual, perhaps early humans acted from **instinct** or learned about sex from watching other species.

. . . .

DID MY PARENTS REALLY DO THAT?
How do I learn to handle that thought?

Because **having sex** is generally an act people do in **private** while they are at least partially naked, it can be wild to imagine people that you know having sex! *It can be especially challenging* when you are just getting used to the whole concept of sex in the first place.

. . . .

Why are grown-ups SO UNCOMFORTABLE talking about sexual intercourse?

There are *a lot of reasons* grown-ups might feel uncomfortable talking about sexual intercourse. Having sex is **private**, intimate, and *usually not something people talk about every day*, so sometimes people have a hard time talking about it. Sometimes parents are nervous that they will be **embarrassed** or say the wrong thing. A lot of parents did not have **conversations** with their own parents about sex, so they don't know about the ways parents and kids can talk about it. Although parents want kids to know about the consequences of sex, sometimes they feel *scared* or *too frightened to speak up even when they feel it's important*. And sometimes they just feel **overwhelmed** by the enormity of the subject—from the mechanics to the consequences, *sex is a big topic!*

What are some sexually translated diseases?

Actually, they are called sexually **transmitted** diseases or infections (STIs), and there are *more than thirty different* STIs that people can get if they are **exposed** to them. All of these infections have similarities and differences. What makes them the same is that they occur from sharing body fluids (like semen and vaginal fluids) during **sexual contact**. What makes them different from one another is how they show up in our bodies and how we treat them. You cannot tell someone has an STI by looking at them, and it is important for you to know how to **protect** yourself from STIs. You and your partner can be tested at any time to see if you have a sexually transmitted infection. When two people make a decision to have sex they also have more conversations about how to keep their bodies safe and healthy. (There is more information about sexually transmitted infections on the other side of the book on pages 79 to 82.)

. . . .

Why do people talk about sex in songs?

People talk about sex in songs because sex is **mysterious**, **interesting**, **passionate**, **challenging**, and a part of many relationships. People use songs *to process their thinking* about things and to tell their stories. Some songs glorify sex and some songs diminish sex and make it ugly. Some people make their songs sexual to make them more **exciting**.

14. Are Hips for Babies to Rest On?

. . . And Other Questions About Pregnancy, Birth Control, Childbirth, and Babies

How long does it take for the SPERM to meet the egg?

When sperm are **released** into the vagina, they use their tails to swim and move around the vagina, into the uterus, and even up into the fallopian tubes. *Sperm can live for days* swimming around. If there is an egg present, as soon as a **single sperm** enters it, the egg is unavailable to the other hundreds of millions of sperm. How long it takes for a single **microscopic** sperm to find a single microscopic egg depends on how fast the sperm swims and where the egg is located—it could take *something like hours*. An egg is considered fertilized when the sperm enters the egg and the two cells become a brand-new single cell. Eggs are often fertilized in the fallopian tubes on their way from the ovaries to the uterus.

Can you make a baby any old time?

People can have sexual intercourse any old time of the day or night; however, there needs to be an egg present for a baby to be conceived, and there is *not always* an egg present outside of an ovary. If the couple having sexual intercourse doesn't want to get pregnant, they need to use birth control (sometimes called contraception). People who make a decision to have sex also need to have conversations about the possibility of pregnancy. There are a lot of conversations that happen with sex!

. . . .

Why do people continue to have sex once they've had a baby and don't want any more babies?

People continue to have sex because it feels good and it's a way to feel connected with their partner—having sex is a way to *show and share your love*. If people do not want to have a baby but do want to have sex, then they need to take responsibility to protect their bodies so they can reduce the chance of an egg and sperm coming together. We call that protection birth control or contraception. There are several ways that people use birth control—one is to not have sex when there is an egg present. Another choice is a covering over the penis called a condom that keeps the sperm inside after it has been released. There are also coverings for the cervix that will keep sperm from entering the uterus. It is also possible for a woman to take additional hormones in the form of a pill, shot, or device inserted under her skin that tells her body *not to release an egg*. There are all sorts of *traditions and beliefs* in cultures and faith groups about contraception. What is essential to know is that if a person with a penis and a person with a vagina are having sexual intercourse, there is always a chance of getting pregnant.

I read in a book that if you have sex standing up you don't get pregnant. Is that true?

You can get pregnant standing, sitting, or lying down. You can get pregnant having sex in a bed, in a car, or on a couch. You can get pregnant if a penis and a vagina are *close enough to touch*.

. . . .

Can you get pregnant other ways besides sexual intercourse? (I've heard sitting on a toilet seat?)

You cannot get pregnant from sitting on a toilet seat, touching a doorknob, shaking hands, or kissing. *You cannot get pregnant unless* a penis gets close to a vagina. Sometimes there is sperm present in fluid on the tip of a penis, and if that touches a woman's vulva *even for a second*, it's possible that sperm would use the fluid available in the vagina to swim inside the woman.

. . . .

If a penis has a CONDOM for sexual intercourse, what's the point of putting the penis inside the vagina because it can't do anything?

Just because a penis has a condom on it doesn't mean that it can't do anything. A condom will help prevent sperm from going into the vagina and reduce the risk of sharing a sexually transmitted infection and starting a pregnancy. It still allows a penis to ejaculate sperm, and the resulting orgasm is very pleasurable.

Where do you get condoms?

Grocery stores and drugstores are typical places people buy CONDOMS and some other kinds of birth control. Some contraception needs a prescription from a health-care provider.

. . . .

Why wouldn't somebody want to have a baby if it's called a miracle?

Getting pregnant and having a baby means a *lot* of love, RESPONSIBILITY, diapers, CRYING, expense, TIME, attention, fun, and worry. There is a *lot* to celebrate when someone has a baby. Babies are WONDERFUL, amazing, lovable, and endearing—however, they require *twenty-four-hour attention and care*, which can be difficult if someone is young or without a job or sick or struggling.

. . . .

How can a whole new life be born in only nine months?

Isn't it amazing? All of the COMPLEX parts of a baby—a heart that can beat, toes that can wiggle—start with two MICROSCOPIC CELLS. Those cells come together to make a brand-new single cell, and from that single cell called a zygote comes the extraordinary YOU! By the way, while it takes a human baby nine months to grow, it takes an elephant baby a year and a half!

Why can't boys have babies?

Men *do* have babies—all the time. Their part in having a baby is to provide the sperm that contributes half of the genetic makeup. The *physical act of carrying a baby* for forty weeks in a uterus and delivering the baby requires female body parts that are perfectly suited for that job. But a partner can be supportive, encouraging, and helpful during pregnancy and childbirth, and do lots of work in caring for the baby after it is born.

. . . .

How does the belly button relate to this?

An umbilical cord connects the baby from its abdomen to the mom's uterus during pregnancy. Made out of a combination of a vein and two arteries, it makes it possible for the *mother's and the baby's blood* to be shared. Every time a pregnant mom takes a breath, oxygen enters her lungs and travels through her body and the umbilical cord so that the baby's body gets the oxygen it needs. Every time the mom takes a bite of a sandwich, that sandwich is digested and all the vitamins, protein, calcium, and other important nutrients travel through her blood and through the umbilical cord so that the baby shares these nourishing things. *When a baby is born,* so is the cord. People assisting in the birth of the baby clamp and cut the cord once the baby is born. The inch or so of cord that remains on the baby dries up and falls off in a few days. The spot *where the cord was originally connected* becomes a belly button.

. . . .

How come some belly buttons go in and some go out? (Mine goes in.)

Not all belly buttons are the same, just like not all feet or elbows are the same. *There is no particular reason* your belly button is a particular size or shape.

If you have sex ten times will you have ten babies?

It is possible to have sex ten times and have ten babies, but those ten times would be spaced around each pregnancy—once a pregnancy starts, having sex doesn't start a new **pregnancy**. Because sperm will not find every egg—and because a woman typically releases a single egg only once a month and it's not always obvious when an egg is present—people *usually* need to have sex **more than** ten times to have ten babies.

. . . .

If you have sex for a very long time will you have twins?

Twins, triplets, or other multiple births do not happen because of the length of time someone has sex. There are two common ways for twins to be conceived. One is when more than one egg is released from the ovaries, so that when millions of sperm are swimming toward the egg, *two* egg/sperm cell combinations are created. These twins are called **fraternal** twins, and they can be two boys, two girls, or a girl and a boy, but they do not look exactly alike because they have two different sets of genetic material. *The second possibility* is that an egg and sperm come together to form a zygote, and then the zygote splits into two groups of cells. Because these two new groups of cells originally came from the same egg/sperm combination and share the exact genetic material, these **identical** twins are almost exactly the same in appearance. *Triplets, quadruplets, and so on* are almost always fraternal.

. . . .

Could I have three babies at one time? P.S. Just say yes or no.

Yes.

Is a baby the funnest thing about having sex?

There are a lot of people who have sex who do not have a baby and call sex fun. In fact, generally people who are having sex have sex many more times than they have babies. Having a baby *is* fun. And having sex is fun too.

. . . .

Does it hurt when you have a baby?
(Just wondering not worried.)

Yes, it does hurt. The uterus works very hard tensing and contracting to push the baby through the vagina. Giving birth also requires the mother to push down with a lot of energy so that she helps the baby *progress through the birth canal.* A mom giving birth often asks people to help her during labor, or strong contractions, by offering her encouraging words, touch, massage, sips of water, and other support. Moms may also ask to receive medicine that can help control the pain. Giving birth is a very powerful physical experience—like climbing a steep mountain—so the mom wants *resources and encouragement* throughout, and will also need time to rest and recover afterward.

. . . .

Is the pregnancy procedure uncomfortable?

Throughout pregnancy, someone might feel excited, nervous, uncomfortable, tired, and energized—a whole range of feelings. When pregnancy feels uncomfortable, the mother might be nauseated, feel pressure on her bladder that makes her need to pee, or have challenges digesting food. *As a baby continues to develop and get bigger*, it will move, kick, and hiccup, which might feel painful or keep the pregnant mom from sleeping well.

Do babies come out head first or feet first? Or does it really matter?

Babies *typically* turn upside down in the uterus a couple of weeks before they are ready to be born, then are born headfirst through the vagina. However, babies *can also be born* feet- or bottom-first. Some babies are born by cesarean section (or C-section). When this happens, a doctor makes a special cut or incision just above the mother's pubic bone through her belly and into her uterus, and the baby is born through that incision. Afterward, the mother's uterus and belly are stitched up by the surgeon.

. . . .

Is giving birth the most PAINFUL AND JOYFUL situation in life?

Yes, *for many people*, giving birth is both painful and joyful. The physical act of labor—the uterus contracting and pushing the baby through the vagina, or having the baby removed by cesarean section—requires the mother to manage her pain. The joyful part is finding out how much your body can do and *welcoming a beautiful baby* into the world.

. . . .

Are hips for babies to rest on?

Yes—*hips are wonderful places for babies to rest*. A woman's hips are usually wider and more prominent than a man's. This means that when a woman is pregnant, her pelvis has the support it needs to hold the uterus as it gets bigger. Her wider hips also *allow the baby to fit through them* as it is being born.

How the heck does the baby fit through the vagina?

Amazing, isn't it? A few things work together to help a baby fit through the vagina and the cervix. First, a baby's skull is more flexible than an older child's. An infant's skull actually consists of several pieces, so that the bones can move together while the baby's head is in a tight space, and then the head expands again after the baby is born. Second, a vagina is quite flexible—it is both *elastic and muscular*—so it can stretch to accommodate a baby's head. The hormones of pregnancy help soften the cervix to make it easier to accommodate a baby. And finally, a woman's hip bones loosen in their sockets to provide more flexibility for the baby to be born.

. . . .

Some people are born with missing senses or qualities that make them different in some other unusual ways. Why is that?

There are many reasons a baby might be born with a physical challenge—from not having the ability to hear to having a foot that is differently shaped. Sometimes babies inherit conditions from their birth parents; sometimes something happens *as the cells divide* and work together to form different body parts. We don't always know the cause for some of the different ways that babies are born. Most people have something unique about their body that makes it different from others, like an unusual birthmark or the way an earlobe is shaped. Maybe you've noticed some of these *characteristics* with your own body.

When you're pregnant, and your baby finally gets ears, can it hear you talking?

There are *tiny little bones* inside the ear canal. Once they are formed, these bones are able to conduct sound by **vibrating** against each other. Of course, babies can't tell us with words what they are hearing. However, some pregnant women can **sense** when a baby appears to move or calm itself *because of certain sounds.*

. . . .

Are you always hungry when you're pregnant? I don't get it, because you give all of the food to the baby.

It is true that during pregnancy, you need more *healthy food* and *calories* to take care of your **body** *plus* a **growing baby**. In places where food is scarce, one of the biggest challenges in delivering healthy, full-size babies is making sure women have **enough to eat**.

. . . .

How do you find out that you are going to have a baby before your uterus gets big?

One of the ways that women notice their bodies are **pregnant** is that they **stop having periods**. During the nine months a woman is pregnant, she does not have a period. Sometimes even before she notices her period has stopped, she experiences nausea or an upset stomach, or she notices that her nipples have darkened in color—*these are additional clues* she might be pregnant.

At what age would it be possible to have a baby? Because I have seen movies about teenagers having babies. So I just wonder.

Once ovaries begin to **release eggs**, it is possible to get **pregnant** if there is sexual contact between a penis and a vagina. You can assume that *once you are in puberty*, it's possible to get pregnant, since there are no flashing lights on our foreheads announcing, "Egg coming!"

. . . .

Are there ways for two lesbian moms to have a baby?

Yes. Two lesbian women (a gay couple of two women) can bring children into their lives through *adoption, foster parenting*, or using a *sperm donor* for conception. Two gay dads can become parents too! Children join families in many wonderful ways—ask your family to tell you the story about the day you came into their lives.

Once the eggs come out, what if you do it again (you know, have sex), where do the new eggs come from? You've already used them. How do you get refills if you want another baby?

You are born with a **million** or so eggs in both ovaries, but *you do not continue to produce eggs* beyond that. You **release an egg** from that original supply of eggs once every period. So women that have more than one baby can have sex again, but they do not need to get "refills"—they release a new egg every month. Women release only a fraction of their eggs over a lifetime.

. . . .

What about donors? I have a donor. They do things slightly a different way.

Most babies are **conceived** (when the egg and sperm come together) through sexual intercourse. There are also babies who are conceived *from an egg or sperm donated by someone*. **In vitro fertilization** is when the cells are brought together in a laboratory by scientists and then implanted as a group of cells into a uterus. It is also possible for donor sperm to be inserted into a vagina to conceive with a woman's egg in her own fallopian tube, which is called **artificial insemination**.

. . . .

What if you do not want a little sister or brother but you get one?

Either way, you are a big sister and that is one of the **best jobs** in the world.

WILL PUBERTY LAST MY WHOLE LIFE?

Why should my body go through puberty if I know I am going to adopt?

We don't have a switch anywhere to turn puberty off or on. And although you may choose to adopt a child when you are older, some of the **other changes** of puberty are part of your body's work to become a grown-up.

What else is there I should know?

It takes a **lifetime** to *learn about our bodies*. Even someone 105 years old has questions about their body! Talking and asking questions about things that make you worried, curious, interested, nervous, excited, and uncertain can take courage. **Learning** about your body gives you information that can help you stay healthy and reassured.

Lots of kids *begin* learning and talking about their bodies with the older people in their lives—parents, grandparents, cousins, and friends. That's probably because those people have had similar experiences growing up, they are familiar, and they are already invested in you. But there are *all sorts* of adults in your life that are interested and invested in helping you grow up well, including teachers, counselors, family friends, coaches, advisors, and health-care providers. When these adults don't have the information you are looking for, they will be able to recommend other resources and experts to provide you with support. **Keep asking and learning**!

Things You Could Ask Grown-Ups

Tell me about the day I became part of our family.

What are some of your favorite things about me?

What are some reasons you're glad you're a grown-up?

Who was the adult you most admired as you were growing up?

How did you figure stuff out when you were going through puberty?

Where did you learn about taking care of yourself, like how to wear deodorant or shave, or how to care for pimples?

Was it easy to talk with your parents? What would have made it easier?

What did you worry about most when you were in puberty, and how did you handle it?

Did you ever have a crush when you were my age? What was that like? Did you tell anyone?

What did people think about being gay when you were a kid?

What did being "popular" mean when you were growing up? Were you ever popular? Did you ever worry about that?

Tell me about a time when you were growing up when you felt different than other people. Did that feeling go away or change as you got older?

What do you remember arguing about most with your family when you were my age? How did you feel when you weren't getting along with your family?

Ideas for Talking to Grown-Ups

WHO: Look for a trusted grown-up in your life who wants puberty to go well for you and wants you to be in healthy, safe, and loving relationships. This could be a family member or a trusted adult like a teacher, doctor or nurse, coach, or counselor.

WHEN: Let a grown-up know you have something on your mind and check in to see when it would work for them to talk.

- When you're watching TV or reading together, you can use the story as a conversation starter: "The kids in this book have some of the same feelings I have . . ."

- When you have a friend or sibling with you that helps you feel more courageous because they share your worry or concern.

WHERE: Sometimes it's easier to be side-by-side when bringing up topics that feel less familiar or uncomfortable, such as:

- Driving in the car or taking a walk together
- Doing an activity like bicycling or hitting golf balls

HOW: Sometimes having conversations about puberty, sex, and growing-up stuff takes more courage than regular conversations. Keeping it simple helps.

- "I've had something on my mind I'd like to talk to you about."
- "I've been worrying about [fill in the blank]. Could we talk about it?"

Will PUBERTY Last My Whole Life?

REAL Answers to REAL Questions from Preteens About Body Changes, Sex, and Other Growing-Up Stuff

Julie Metzger, RN, MN, and Robert Lehman, MD

Illustrated by Lia Cerizo

little bigfoot
an imprint of sasquatch books
seattle, wa

Contents

Introduction

Welcome to the book of questions asked by preteen **boys** (and girls—turn over and see the girls' side)!

Who is asking these questions, you might wonder? Julie Metzger and Rob Lehman have been leading classes for preteen **boys** and preteen **girls** (and a parent or other trusted adult) on **puberty** and **growing-up** issues for more than thirty years. During these classes, we invite the preteens to ask **questions** on note cards so that we can answer them for the whole group, and we've saved every one of them. We've included some of the most frequently asked questions (*with a sprinkling of ones that made us smile*).

Though these are all actual questions asked by **preteens**, we invite parents (yes, *especially* parents!) and educators and anyone else interested in what's on the minds of kids to read through these questions and our answers. Our responses are not meant to be exhaustive or the final word. Throughout the book we've tried to **encourage** kids to continue discussing these subjects in **conversations** with their parents and/or trusted adults. We believe that *families should be* the primary sexuality educators of children, and if these questions generate more questions, that's great.

Any differences you see between the boys' and the girls' sides reflect many years of answering preteens' questions and realizing that boys and girls may approach things **differently**. Hopefully we stay true to the tone that resonates with each gender. We also realize that many questions are common to all preteens, and that gender identity is more fluid than what our culture once assumed—this edition embraces both of those ideas.

Our most grateful thanks to all the preteens who were **brave** enough to submit a question and curious enough to sit through our classes and talk about subjects that were obviously important to them.

Thanks to our colleagues who reviewed the material to keep us **honest**, the kids who reviewed the material to keep us developmentally on-target, and our friends and families who made sure it stayed **interesting**.

And thanks *most of all* to my spouse, Christopher, for his unending support; to my mom, Roz Lehman, who inspired me to write even though she couldn't be here to see it; and my dad, Ed Lehman, who is still around to show his pride and love for his family, and here for us to love him back.

This second edition covers some new areas we didn't address in our first book and uses language that is more inclusive for all preteens.

Dr Rob

ROBERT LEHMAN, MD

Robert Lehman, MD, has devoted his professional career to adolescent health care. As a physician, his practice has focused on teenagers in several different clinical situations; he has worked for many years as an advocate for youth on the local and national levels; and as a member of the faculty at University of Washington, he has dedicated himself to teaching about adolescent health-care needs to various health-care professionals, parents, adolescents, and many other groups. For over thirty years, he and Julie Metzger have led classes for the public to promote parent-child communication about sexuality and other issues of adolescence through Great Conversations. For more information on classes, programs, and other resources, visit GreatConversations.com.

great **conversations**
about growing up. together.

1. Will **Puberty** Last My Whole Life?

... And Other Questions About Puberty

What exactly is puberty? Can you feel puberty?

Puberty is the time when your body (and your *thoughts and emotions* too!) goes through all sorts of **changes**, mostly in your preteen and teenage years. *Can you feel it?* Not exactly, but you certainly can see that it's happening. Puberty is the time when your body changes from a **boy's** to a **man's**. It's set to start just like an alarm clock. At a certain age (determined by what you inherited from your birth mother and birth father), a message from your **brain** gives the signal. It tells a gland just under your brain, called the pituitary, to make a lot of a certain chemical, or **hormone**, that then travels all over your body. When it gets to your testicles, which are glands themselves, it tells them to make another hormone, called **testosterone**. This then *flows all through your body*, telling different parts to do different things—it tells your bones to grow faster, making you **taller**; it tells your muscles to get bigger and **stronger**; it tells your skin to grow **hair** in new places and produce oil; and it tells your voice box to grow longer, making your voice get lower. When you're all done, you will *look, act, and think like a* **man**.

1

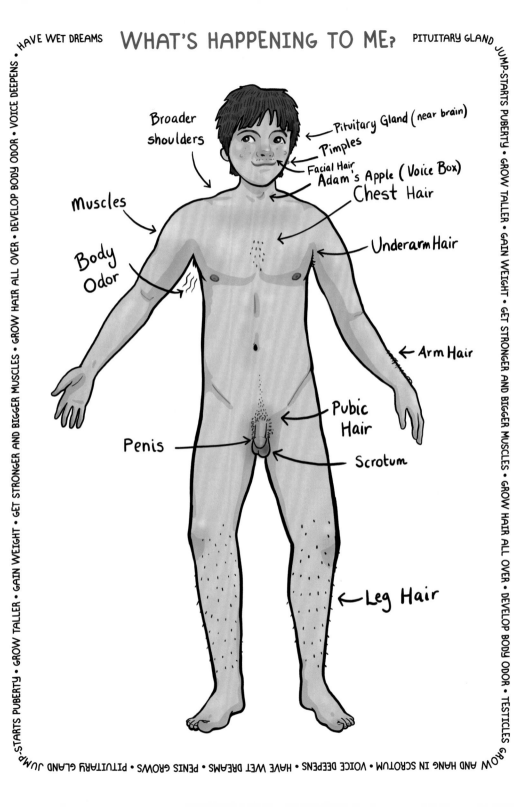

WHAT'S HAPPENING TO ME?

Broader shoulders

Pituitary Gland (near brain)

Pimples

Facial Hair

Adam's Apple (Voice Box)

Chest Hair

Muscles

Underarm Hair

Body Odor

Arm Hair

Pubic Hair

Penis

Scrotum

Leg Hair

HAVE WET DREAMS • VOICE DEEPENS • DEVELOP BODY ODOR • GROW HAIR ALL OVER • GET STRONGER AND BIGGER MUSCLES • GAIN WEIGHT • GROW TALLER • JUMP-STARTS PUBERTY

PITUITARY GLAND

JUMP-STARTS PUBERTY • GROW TALLER • GAIN WEIGHT • GET STRONGER AND BIGGER MUSCLES • GROW HAIR ALL OVER • DEVELOP BODY ODOR • TESTICLES GROW AND HANG IN SCROTUM • PENIS GROWS • HAVE WET DREAMS • VOICE DEEPENS • PITUITARY GLAND JUMP-STARTS PUBERTY

How big is a HORMONE?

A hormone is a **chemical**. *You can't see it*, but it is carried by your blood to all parts of your body, including your **brain**, which also changes during puberty. Puberty starts when a lot of this hormone, called **testosterone**, gets released by the testicles and causes *all these amazing changes*.

. . . .

Is it WEIRD going through puberty?

Some people wish they could stay just the way they were as kids, while others can't wait to **grow up**. The thing is, **everyone** goes through puberty and has to experience the same changes. You might think that all this is **weird** because it's new, but you can be certain that *it's normal*—everyone else is doing it too.

. . . .

I wonder when I will have PUBERTY. I wonder if it will be hard.

Most boys start puberty between the ages of ten and twelve, though a few can start earlier and a few later—and all of them are **normal**. The first thing you'll see is pubic hair, the hair growing around your penis. The next place you'll see hair is in your armpits, then on your arms, legs, and other places, with your full beard not coming in until much later. In the meantime, you'll be **growing** taller, getting bigger **muscles**, and developing a lower voice. It might be confusing, surprising, or even astounding, but it's not hard—it's normal and *everybody goes through it*! (Girls' puberty is slightly different in timing and other things—for information, see the girls' side!)

What if I don't feel like all the other boys?

There could be *many reasons* to feel that way. Sometimes it's because you're experiencing puberty earlier or later, or slower or faster than the other boys you know. You might feel different from them, even though you're all **normal**. It could be because you're attracted to boys, or both boys and girls, or no one right now. And sometimes, a kid who is born with boy reproductive parts doesn't feel like a "boy" inside—maybe they feel more like a girl, or a mix of boy and girl, or maybe they feel *really confused* about the whole gender thing. When we feel different, we tend to keep those things to ourselves and worry about them a lot. Try talking to a **trusted adult** about what makes you feel different. You'll probably find there are others who feel the same way as you. And that in itself can make you feel a whole lot better.

. . . .

Can I still do things that I like to do (like building models)?

When your **body**—and the rest of you—**grows up**, you will naturally get interested in a lot of **new things**. Just because you add new interests doesn't mean you have to lose all the old ones.

. . . .

A question I have is how much will I be like my dad?

We **inherit** most of what we are from our birth mothers and birth fathers—hair color, height, foot size, good looks, and lots of other things—but we are *a mix of both* of their **families**. So some of us take after one more than the other and some of us look like a little bit of both. But we are more than just what we inherit. We are **influenced** by our friends, by what we learn, and *by our experiences*—all of these things help make us **unique** individuals.

Why is puberty so EMBARRASSING?

Maybe puberty **feels** embarrassing because it has a lot to do with our **bodies**, and there are some parts of our bodies that we don't talk about very much, so it takes some getting used to. Maybe puberty feels embarrassing also because it's **new** and *because it happens no matter what*. Hopefully, after reading all these questions asked by other kids your age, it will be **a little less** embarrassing for you.

. . . .

Is it OK to talk about this with my friends?

You bet. In fact, show them this book! You should also talk about this stuff with your **parents** or other trusted adults in your life—after all, they've definitely gone through this themselves and can help you **understand** and get through the changes that are coming. They want this to go well for you. The more you talk about **growing up** and the more questions you ask about it, the **less scary** it will seem. Here's a *fun exercise you can do*: ask a parent or other adult in your life to name three things that make them glad they're grown up. The more adults you ask, the more things you'll learn to *look forward* to as you grow up yourself.

. . . .

How do you know if you're NORMAL?

It's **normal** to worry about *whether you're normal*! Boys, men, girls, and women all think about this. Your friends might be a little ahead of or a little behind you as they progress through puberty, but "normal" includes all of these paths to **growing up**. Some boys look at their friends or other boys at school and wonder why they seem to be so far ahead in **puberty**, or why they look so **different**. Throughout your preteen and teen years, you might see others who are taller or more muscular than you. Remember that the timing of puberty for you is set by what you *inherit from your birth parents*—not everyone starts at the same time or goes at the same speed. You could be the exact same age as another person but be at a different

place in puberty. That's OK—you'll all be adults in time. This is a terrific example of being *different but normal*. And, if you're one of those boys who is progressing a little later than his friends, the good news is that you might continue growing even after they've stopped. So you might wind up taller than them in the long run!

. . . .

Will puberty last my WHOLE LIFE?

Puberty is over when you no longer grow any taller. *For the average guy,* that's at about age eighteen, though some can stop sooner while others can continue **growing** after high school. (Girls tend to start earlier and end sooner than boys.) But being a grown-up is a totally different thing, since it also involves the **responsibilities** of an adult. *And guess what?* Although puberty ends near the end of our teen years, our bodies (and minds!) continue to change throughout our lives. So you're not the only one growing and changing in the house—*everyone is.*

When do I get to look like **THAT?**

2. Do **Growth** **Spurts** Hurt?

. . . And Other Questions About Growing Taller

How tall will I GROW?

How tall you grow depends on what you **inherited** from your birth mother and birth father. If you know your birth families on both sides, you can take a look at the adults and get a good idea of how tall you'll be. If one side of the family is **short** and the other is **tall**, you might be right in the middle, or closer to one or the other. Boys tend to *follow their birth dads* a little bit more closely than their birth moms. And if you don't know your birth parents on both sides, that's OK—you'll just have to be surprised, but you will probably wind up about average anyway. Another way to know is to ask your doctor or medical provider—they have something called a **growth chart**. It shows dots for each height as you are growing up, and they can predict fairly well how tall you'll be when you're fully grown.

Oh, and don't worry if your friends are growing faster than you—*you'll catch up.* The great news is that no matter what your final height is, you'll still be a **normal** grown-up person.

Does diet pop and soda and coffee STUNT your growth?

No. People have blamed lots of things for making them shorter than they wanted to be, but none of these by themselves can be blamed for that. Although some boys can have major health problems that may affect their **height**, how tall most boys grow is determined by their genetic **inheritance** from their parents. Getting good **nutrition**, *plenty of exercise*, and enough **sleep** will all help you to get as tall as your family genetics will allow.

. . . .

Why are girls usually shorter than boys?

Height is just another one of the differences *between males and females*—in general, grown **women** are not as tall as grown **men**. That's not to say you don't see very tall women or very short men—you do. And since girls usually start puberty a couple years before boys do and finish it faster (check it out on page 3 in the girls' section), you might find girls looking much taller or older than you when you're twelve or thirteen. But eventually boys will hit their *growth spurts* and catch up.

. . . .

Do growth spurts hurt?

No! A **growth spurt** is that period of puberty when you appear to others to be *growing faster than a weed*. But it isn't that fast, and it **doesn't hurt** a bit. If you're an active guy, you might get **growing pains** (nighttime aches in your lower legs) early in puberty, but they go away as you continue to grow.

At what age do you STOP GROWING?

The **average** guy stops growing around age **eighteen**, or during his senior year of high school. But that means half of all guys might stop sooner, while half continue to grow after high school. We stop **growing** because the same **hormone** that makes us grow faster in puberty (*testosterone*, remember?) also helps finish up that growing. Once you're done, *you're done*. You'll still make testosterone for all the other things you need it for, but it won't make you grow any more.

3. How Come I Go to McDonald's a Lot but Don't Get Bigger?

. . . And Other Questions About Growing Bigger Muscles

When do guys start getting BIGGER MUSCLES?

Actually, your muscles have been growing, just like all the other parts of your body, *since you were born*. But when puberty starts and your body makes lots of testosterone, your muscles will grow faster and stronger than ever. It can start somewhat slowly; at the beginning of puberty your body wants to get taller more than anything else. But when you get near the end of puberty and are not growing much taller anymore, you'll see your muscles change *a lot more*.

. . . .

Will I be STRONGER if I exercise?

Absolutely! Your muscles will need three things to get as big and strong as they can: a lot of good nutrition, those puberty hormones (like testosterone), and exercise. If you exercise, your muscles will get toned (that means they will be able to handle increased demands and be less likely to get strained). If you want to build them even bigger, then you'll need to do specific exercises for those

muscles. Runners develop different muscles than gymnasts, and gymnasts will be different than baseball players. *Your heart is a muscle too*, and you can exercise it by doing most any activity that makes it beat faster. Different sports or exercises can have different effects on the strength, flexibility, coordination, and bulk of various muscles.

If you don't eat enough nutritional food but work out a lot, will you still GET BIG MUSCLES?

That would be like building a house with a lot of workers but not enough bricks or lumber! In order to **build** big muscles, you have to give them the **nutrients** they need. This certainly includes **protein**, but not *only* protein—it takes all the nutrients that you get from a *balanced diet*. Luckily, the testosterone that helps you build these muscles is also going to give you a larger appetite to make sure you take in what you need.

How come I go to McDonald's a lot but don't get BIGGER?

Just because you eat a lot of food doesn't mean you're eating the best **balance** of food. Try asking your parents to find out what *the best combination of foods* is for you that will help you **grow** to your max. You need protein, carbohydrates, fats, minerals, vitamins, fiber, and water, but the amounts of each depend on your age, how much you're growing, what activities you're involved with, and even the body type you inherited from your birth families. You and your parents can also ask your doctor or medical provider for advice on what you need, and there are plenty of books and internet resources for that information too. **Fast food** restaurants do have some good choices, but they can also have some unhealthy ones—lower-calorie options might be better than

high-calorie things with lots of gooey cheese and bacon on them. And remember, if you eat too many **calories** but *don't exercise enough*, it might be your waist that grows more than your height or your muscles!

. . . .

Is it bad to lift weights?

It depends. When you're just starting puberty, a lot of **weight lifting** won't do so much for your muscles, since your body is putting most of its efforts into *growing taller*. Also this is a time when the growing parts of your **bones** (around your knees for your legs and at your shoulders and wrists for your arms) can potentially get **injured**. Lifting the *wrong way* or lifting *too much* weight too early could harm these growth centers. Waiting until later in puberty, such as high school, makes weight training more effective and safer. If you want to lift weights, don't just do it on your own—ask a **coach** or **trainer** for the proper and safe way to do it for the muscles you want to tone up.

. . . .

Is it true that STEROIDS will really make your muscles bigger?

If you're talking about **muscle-building** steroids (and not some of the other kinds that people use to treat conditions like asthma), it's true. Combined with exercise, *they do build muscle.* But there are some major-league **problems** with using these types of steroids. I can think of five right off the top of my head: they are expensive, they hurt (since most need to be given by a shot), they are unfair in competition, they're **illegal**, and they can cause lots of bad **side effects** (like severe acne or a sick liver). So they may work, but they surely *don't seem worth it.*

What I Most Look Forward to About Being a Grown-Up

- Getting a bigger brain
- To get bigger, smarter, and stronger than my parents
- Mustache
- Becoming the CEO of Microsoft
- Being awesome
- Being done with puberty
- Doing things that parents get to do, like watching cool movies
- Eating a ton (even though I already do)
- Muscles, so I can take on my older brother
- Getting a Lamborghini
- No mom to boss me around
- Girls

4. Will You Burp Deeper?

. . . And Other Questions About Voice Change

I heard that your voice will change and go down, but that sometimes it will crack and go up. Why?

Along with all the other things that grow during puberty, your **voice box** (or *larynx*) gets longer too. The longer it gets, the **lower** the sound is when air moves through it. It's just like with instruments: tall bassoons have a lower sound than short clarinets, and long trombones sound much deeper than short trumpets. In fact, the voice box gets so big in guys that you can see its top end poking out on the front of your neck—some people call this the *Adam's apple*, though it doesn't look much like an apple to me. When you make **testosterone**, your voice box grows, and your voice sounds deeper. As for the voice **cracking**—anyone who is first learning how to play an instrument knows it takes time to get the sound right. Boys with voice boxes that are just starting to grow have to get used to that new sound going through—eventually the up-and-down cracking stops and people will be surprised at how **low** your voice sounds. Some guys will have very **deep** voices and could sing as basses, while other guys will have **higher** voices and could sing as tenors—and *there's everything in between*. Oh, and tall guys can have higher voices and shorter guys can have really deep ones. You'll only know what your voice will sound like *when you're done with puberty* and try it out.

How long does it take for your voice to change?

The **voice** starts to change not long after puberty begins, but it might be difficult to notice early on. Sometimes, in the course of a year, a guy can have a dramatic **change** in his voice but it's hard for him to notice *since he hears himself every day*. It's usually when Aunt Tillie visits and makes a comment about how grown-up you sound, or when you hear yourself on a recording, that you really take notice. Your voice is usually done changing *before you finish growing taller*.

Will you burp deeper?

Well, when a baby burps, it sounds **softer** and higher pitched than when a **grown man** does it, so maybe you're right—but *that might come from* the man having a bigger stomach and longer distance for the burp to come out, not because he has a longer voice box.

Why does your voice change when you get flabbier?

Things *other than puberty* can affect how your voice sounds. Some people find that gaining a lot of weight can make the voice sound **different**. Some notice that eating or drinking certain things, such as milk, can also affect it. Some people get **training** to make their voice sound better. One boy I knew tried to hurry up his voice change by standing in front of a mirror and practicing talking really deeply. It didn't work. I told him that his voice change would *definitely come all on its own*, just like the rest of puberty.

5. Does **Pubic Hair** Hurt When It Grows?

. . . And Other Questions About Body Hair

Where does the FIRST adolescent hair usually grow?

You'll usually first notice the hair that grows around your penis, which is commonly called your **pubic** area. Hair will eventually grow from your genitals (penis and scrotum) up to your belly button and *down to your thighs*. If you're really looking forward to all the body changes of puberty, that's the first place to look. Some boys can start to grow hair when they're as young as ten and some not until they're fourteen, but *they're all normal*. You might notice the hair starts out fairly straight and later gets somewhat **curly**. It also starts just at the base of the penis and later can show up on the legs and belly and even the butt, but those places can vary depending on how **hairy** you wind up being. After the pubic area, the second place hair usually grows is in your **armpits**, and after that, on the rest of your body.

Does pubic hair hurt when it grows?

Not at all. Some boys might be amazed at it, while some boys might think it looks weird. Still others will hardly notice. But everyone grows it as part of growing up. An occasional guy might wonder if people ever **shave** this hair off—yes, they can, but like other body hair, it will grow back and be a little **itchy** as it starts to regrow. And yes, girls grow pubic hair too but in a slightly different pattern.

. . . .

Why do we have pubic hair anyway?

No one knows for sure. Think of how we **evolved** from species that were much hairier than we are, just like chimps and other primates are now. The species we evolved from were covered with hair *from top to bottom,* but we've lost that hair because we didn't need it—that's why we don't have hair on our elbows or knees. Why didn't the hair in our pubic area also go away? Some think it plays a role in making us more sexually **attractive** or in causing less **friction** down there, while some think it's to **protect** our genitals. *This might always be a mystery.*

. . . .

Does hair grow ON MY BUTT or is that a myth and is it a disease?

When guys go through puberty, hair can **grow** in *lots of places* it didn't before, such as your arms, legs, chest, back, the backs of your hands, the tops of your feet, and even on your butt. But some guys grow **very little** hair and some guys grow **a lot.** It's all normal, but the amount of hair you'll grow depends on how **hairy** your birth families are on both sides. Oh, and you'll grow hair in your nose and ears too. *Isn't that amazing?*

What I Least Look Forward to in Growing Up

- Taxes, paperwork, and complicated grown-up things
- Hair in the pubic zone
- Looking weird and oldish
- Everything; I don't want to grow up; I really like my childhood, and I want to enjoy the ride while it lasts
- Life (the bad bits)
- Getting wrinkly and gray hairs and three-digit age
- Being by myself and not knowing everything
- Being the one with responsibilities, being the one that people look up to, and not having someone to turn to
- The first job interview and the first date
- Girls

How come some kids get MORE HAIR than others?

You **inherit** the amount of hair you're going to have from your birth mother and birth father. If you know both sides of your family, you can look at them (the guys on both sides) to see about how **hairy** you're going to be. If they're really hairy on both sides, you're probably going to be too. If they're hardly hairy at all, then you probably won't be either. And if the guys on one side of your family are hairy and the guys on the other side aren't, you could be like one side or the other, or right in the middle. If you don't know both sides of your family (lots of guys don't for many reasons), *you can bet you're going to be pretty normal* with your hair. Oh, and the amount of hair on a guy has nothing to do with how manly he is—a guy's manliness is only determined by how he thinks, acts, and feels.

. . . .

Can you get TOO HAIRY on your arms and legs?

Unlike hair on your head and hair on your face, which will get longer and longer if you don't cut it, hair on other parts of your body just tends to **stop** at a certain **length**, depending on where it is. So you really don't have to worry that you'll have to comb your arms and legs too!

. . . .

Why on earth do we have hair in our ears?

Great question! A lot of guys wonder about this. Some people think that we have hair in our ears to **prevent** dirt from getting in there and clogging them up—just like nose hair helps to prevent dust from getting into our noses and possibly our lungs. But most guys think that ear hair is just **annoying**. Both men and women get nose hair, but it's mostly only guys who get ear hair. *Lucky us!*

Why do you get facial hair? When does it grow?

The same **hormone** that makes us grow taller, get bigger muscles, and have lower voices (*testosterone*) also makes hair grow during puberty in certain places it never grew before. Your **face** is just one of those places. Your **facial hair** starts to grow when puberty begins but it doesn't come in fully until much later—for some guys, not until their twenties! Some guys will grow hair early, while some will grow it later; some guys will wind up having a lot, while others won't have as much; some will have dark hair, while some will have very light hair. A lot of these differences depend on what you **inherit** from your birth parents, so you'll probably end up looking *a lot like the men in your family.*

. . . .

Does SHAVING affect hair growth anywhere (not just your face)?

Although lots of boys might think that shaving speeds up hair growth, that's a **myth**. Shaving hair makes no difference in how fast it's going to grow back—whether that's on your head, your face, or anywhere else. *Hair is on its own schedule.*

Will your beard grow your hair color?

Usually. Sometimes it can be a little **lighter** or **darker**, and when you get old, it can turn gray earlier or later than the rest of your hair. The color has a lot to do with your family and what color hair you inherited from your birth mom and birth dad. Oh, and the hair of your beard *might feel a little different* from the hair on your head.

. . . .

How do you grow a GOATEE?

Easy! You **shave** away everything that isn't a goatee! *The good thing is*, if you don't like what you see, you can always let it **grow out** or shave it off.

. . . .

When will I have to begin shaving?

Many boys will see *some soft hair growing* above their **upper lips** early in puberty. You can start shaving as soon as you have hair to shave. One of the cool things about facial hair is that you can **decide** what you want it to look like . . . and change your mind. Do you want a clean-shaven face, or do you want a long **beard**? Or maybe a **mustache** you can twist around your ears?! You can try something out, like a soul patch, then shave it off if you don't want it anymore.

Can I completely GET RID OF facial hair?

Though it might be **annoying** to have to shave all the time, there's really **no way** to stop facial hair from growing as long as your testicles are making testosterone. Think of it as *just part of being a guy*. Some people who want to get rid of facial hair (or hair anywhere) can choose to use methods such as waxing, which is temporary, or laser, which is permanent, but since these methods can be very uncomfortable and/or expensive, it's important to consider that compared to the inconvenience of shaving.

. . . .

If you have a light beard, will shaving it off and starting again make it come in thicker?

That's a **myth**! Shaving early or shaving a lot will not make your beard grow **faster**, or **thicker**, or better. *Don't bother shaving* if there's nothing there to shave yet! It will grow in eventually, so *be patient*. Some guys inherit really thick beards from their families, while other guys have very light beards that don't need to be shaved as often. Just be patient—many guys don't start getting their full adult beards until their twenties.

. . . .

How do you do it (I mean SHAVING)?

You can choose a **razor blade** (check out all the types there are in a drugstore) or an **electric shaver**. You can shave dry, but using something to lubricate your skin first (like water, soap, or shaving cream) can help keep you from cutting yourself. Then you can choose where to start and which way to move the razor, though *you'll learn which way cuts better* as you go along. A great way to learn is to watch your dad or uncle or grandfather or any **grown-up guy** you feel close to. See what he does and ask him why he shaves that way. And by the way, many women shave parts of their bodies too, and they can also teach you about shaving.

What is the point of aftershave?

I've wondered about that myself! In the old days when razors weren't as well made and men routinely *cut themselves* while shaving, products like aftershave were splashed on to prevent infections and perhaps to help cuts heal faster. These days, both razor blades and electric shavers rarely nick your skin, so I suppose it's more to make you smell nice.

. . . .

Is there a way to STOP the hair on my body?

Some people don't like the hair that *grows* with puberty because they like their bodies the way they are, some people remove body hair because they feel it *looks better* or is *fashionable,* and some remove hair because they are active in certain sports, such as competitive swimming. You inherit the amount of hair you get from your birth parents, but you get to make the choice of how to manage it throughout your life.

. . . .

Why do men go bald?

Some men inherit the tendency to lose the hair on their heads from their families. Scientists are still trying to figure this out—it has something to do with one's hormones and how they act on one's hair—and they haven't figured out how to completely stop it yet. Luckily, men can look great even with little or no hair. But if you're still concerned about it, maybe they'll discover a way to *stop balding* by the time you grow up.

6. How **Smelly** Will I Get?

. . . And Other Questions About Body Odor

How does BODY ODOR start?

Body odor is another one of those things we all face when we grow up. When the **testosterone** starts pumping through your body to make you taller and stronger, it also changes your skin. Not only does your skin grow hair in certain places, it also produces more **oil** and **sweat**. Oil keeps our skin from getting too dry and sweat *keeps us from getting too hot*. But sometimes we make too much oil and too much sweat. When that happens, the **bacteria** on our skin (which have always lived there but haven't caused trouble) start to multiply as they feast on all that oil and sweat. It's the bacteria that make that very interesting odor.

Armpits smell particularly bad because they have many **sweat glands** and **oil glands**, and are nice dark places where **bacteria** like to grow. There are other similar places on your body—*like your feet and your pubic area*—where bacteria like to grow too. But many guys just seem to smell bad all over.

How SMELLY will I get?

Your odor is very individual, and it's affected by how active you are and what you do about it. But let's just say that teenagers can get pretty smelly. Some boys wonder why they can't tell how smelly they are. Our noses become accustomed to a bad smell if it's there all the time. So you might have to *rely on someone else to let you know* when you start smelling bad. Don't ask your friend to put their nose in your armpit! Don't ask your dog—they love you no matter how bad you stink. And definitely don't ask your first date—not if you ever expect a second one! Ask someone who cares about you and is good at picking up odors, like a parent or another adult with whom you live.

Unlike acne, which tends to get better when you grow up, *body odor is something all active people* have to deal with their whole lives. The more active you are, the more you'll need to watch for body odor. Most adults take showers daily and use some form of deodorant, but you can make that decision for yourself when you reach adulthood.

How do you tell a friend they need deodorant?

You can tell him what you learned to help with your own body odor. First, the best thing is to wash off as much of the sweat, oil, and bacteria as you can. That means a *shower or bath* with soap. But some guys need something more, such as deodorant or antiperspirant. These are products you can buy in a grocery store or drugstore that you rub in your armpits to cover up the smell. They come in many different scents and styles. Antiperspirants not only cover up your smell, but also have a chemical in them called aluminum that stops you from sweating for a while. It's best for guys just starting puberty to stick

with washing when they start to smell. Guys further along in puberty might want to use deodorants or, later in teenage years, antiperspirants. If you're curious, *ask your parents* what they use and why they chose it. I'm sure your **strong-smelling** friend will get the message after hearing your advice.

7. What is the Point of Getting Zits?

. . . And Other Questions About Pimples

What is the point of getting zits?

No one gets zits because they want to, and zits serve **no useful purpose** to my knowledge! But I can tell you *how we get them*. That same hormone, **testosterone**, that boys make so much of in puberty, causes a lot of changes in their bodies. One of these changes is that your skin makes more **oil**—more oil than you need to keep your skin healthy. Your skin makes so much oil that you can see it on your forehead and other places as the day goes on. This oil tends to fill in tiny holes in your skin, called **pores**, which blocks them, resulting in bumps we call **pimples**, *acne*, or *zits*.

Does everyone FOR SURELY get acne?

There is hardly a **grown-up** who didn't have at least some **pimples** at some time in their life. Some people will have only a few while others can get **a lot**. Although the tendency to have acne generally runs in families, other things can determine if you'll get a lot of **acne** or just a little—so looking at your brother or sister or asking your birth parents if they had bad acne probably won't predict exactly how yours will be. *The important thing* is that nothing can keep you from ever having

a zit, no matter what they say in a television commercial. What you need to do is **take care of** your skin when you have zits so that your *face looks as good as before* when they eventually go away.

. . . .

What are BLACK- AND WHITEHEADS?

Once your **pores** get *blocked with oil*, the stuff inside the zit can build up (making it look **white** or **black**) or get infected (making it look red and feel tender). Sometimes an infected zit will need a special medicine, but mostly these pimples just need to be **cared for** (see page 30).

. . . .

Is acne only on your face?

That's the place people care about most, since it's the place that's *most obvious to others*. But you can get **acne** on your shoulders, back, chest, and even on your thighs. In fact, you can get zits anywhere, but these are the usual trouble spots.

. . . .

Do any foods make acne WORSE?

Although *lots of people might think so*, it's not fully understood how foods could make acne **worse**. People might get that idea because certain foods (like nuts and candy) have a lot of oils in them, and it's oil on your skin that causes acne. But the **oils** in food and the oil on your skin are *different*. The truth is that your **skin** makes the acne-causing oil no matter how much or little oil you are eating in your food, mostly because it's primarily a result of the **hormones** you produce in puberty.

What happens when you have a zit at school and a girl is grossed out?

Some people are embarrassed by their zits and think everyone is staring at them. They'll try things like combing their hair over their foreheads (that could make it worse!) or covering their faces with some cream to hide the zits (if the cream contains oil, that could also make it worse!). Remember, *everyone gets zits* at some point or another. So the best thing to do is to take care of your zits and try to keep from getting too many of them (see page 30). And, by the way, *girls get zits too* (see page 17 on the girls' side).

Did you play any sports in high school or college that made you get acne?

You're probably asking that because you heard that sports can make acne worse. Well, it's not the sports, actually, but the helmets you wear while you play sports that *can cause your skin to make even more oil*. The key is washing your face after practice to make sure that wearing a helmet doesn't make things worse.

If you don't wash your face will zits STAY FOREVER?

No, zits will eventually go away. The main reason to take care of your skin is to prevent zits from getting infected, because when a zit gets infected, it can lead to scarring. Scars are those marks or pits you see on some grown-ups even though they no longer have any zits. You can make your zits better, but you can't get rid of those scars.

At what age do zits go away?

Sorry to tell you, but *grown-ups can get zits too*. But the good news is that they'll be much less of a problem when you finish puberty, so take the time during puberty to really **take care of your skin** so that it looks good later.

. . . .

Does TOOTHPASTE remove zits?

No, it doesn't (but it does a good job on your teeth!). You might hear of a lot of things kids have tried to make their acne better, but most of them don't work. The first thing you need to do is get rid of as much of that **oil** as possible. **Washing your face** once or twice a day with water and soap (any soap—it doesn't have to be fancy), either at the sink or in the shower or bath, will be the absolute best thing for reducing pimples. If you're doing that but you are still getting zits, then go to the store or pharmacy with your parent and pick up an **acne medicine**. Check out the ingredients for something called *benzoyl peroxide* 5 percent, or just BP 5 percent, which is the most important thing to help your pimples. Something called *salicylic acid* can also be useful. If the medicine has alcohol or a ton of other chemicals but neither of these chemicals, then it might not help your face no matter how much it costs. And, if you're washing daily and using one of these products and you're still getting a lot of pimples, then you can ask a doctor or nurse practitioner to prescribe a **more powerful** medicine to help you. But most kids don't need anything like this if they *simply wash their faces* and use the products mentioned above.

8. Does Food Affect Your Penis Size?

. . . And Other Questions About Your Penis and Erections

How and why do penises grow?

From the time you're born, *your body is growing*. When you enter puberty, everything grows even faster. That includes your penis as well as almost all of the other parts of you. You might notice your penis getting a little longer at first, then eventually a little wider—but most boys don't notice much change until one day they take a look and wonder, "Wow! When did that happen?" You might also notice other changes in this area, including hair growing around your penis, your testicles getting bigger, and your scrotum (the sac holding the testicles) getting darker. All of this is totally normal, and I'll explain it further on.

When does a penis STOP GROWING and reach its top size?

Usually when you stop growing taller, which is the end of puberty, your penis stops growing too. For most boys, that's at the end of high school, but the exact timing can vary. Some things (like your beard, see page 20) can still continue to change even after you stop growing.

Does PENIS SIZE matter?

A *lot* of guys spend *too much* time worrying about whether their penis is big enough. Actually, your penis will be absolutely the right size to do the things it's supposed to do—urinate and have sex (more on that later!). Some guys might think that having a bigger penis makes you manlier, but *that's not true at all*. Other guys might think that you'll be more popular if you have an enormous penis, but popularity has nothing to do with penis size. Besides, what would you do with a four-foot-long penis anyway?! You might hear people say they have some surefire way to make your penis bigger faster. *Don't believe them*! Your penis will grow in its own time. Don't worry—yours will be normal and do what it needs to do.

. . . .

Does food affect your penis size?

Nope. Nor does pulling on it, making wishes, or changing the type of underwear you wear! It will get as *big as it will get*, and it will work just fine.

. . . .

Why does my penis look DIFFERENT from some other guys'?

Well, it could have to do with circumcision. Check out the picture (page 40) so that this makes sense. Every guy in the world is born with a thin piece of skin that covers the tip of his penis (called a foreskin). Some parents choose to have this piece of skin removed soon after birth by a doctor or a religious person. If this happens, we call it a *circumcised* penis. Otherwise, it's an *uncircumcised* penis. Some parents choose circumcision because it's a religious custom, some do it because they *think it's healthier*, and some choose to circumcise the baby boy because the dad is circumcised and the parents want the son to look the same.

If a boy isn't circumcised, will it affect his life?

Like we talked about previously, *penises are designed to do two things*: to **pee** and to **have sex**. Whether you are circumcised or not, your penis will be able to do both of these things just fine. Millions of boys still have their foreskins and millions don't. The only thing is, if you still have a foreskin, it's good to **clean** underneath it when taking a shower or bath (just like cleaning any other part of your body). Slide the foreskin back as much as it will go comfortably, clean underneath, then let it go back where it was. *Easy*!

. . . .

Is it painful to have a circumcision when you're 16 years old?

It hurts any time part of your body gets cut. *When it's done on babies*, sometimes the doctor will numb the area first, but babies are very forgiving and forget very quickly, since the cut heals up fast. In some cases (again because of tradition or because of an unusual medical problem with the foreskin) boys may get a circumcision when they're older. Usually, these boys are **asleep** for this surgery or numbed really well.

. . . .

When I rub my penis, I get a STRANGE FEELING. Why?

You also might notice that your penis **changes shape** when you do this. Let me explain. You might think that **erections** have only to do with sex, but boys get erections *even before they're born*! You have special nerve endings around your penis that, when touched in a certain way, signal special openings in your penis to fill with blood, causing it to get bigger, **harder**, and point upward. We call that an erection or an erect penis. When you stop touching the penis, the extra blood

leaves, and your penis goes back to the shape it was before. Baby boys get erections when their diapers go on and off, and young boys get them occasionally when washing their penises. But when a guy gets to puberty, the whole thing gets super sensitive—almost anything can make the penis erect. Erections can happen at any time—when you're in class, when you're reading, or when you're simply staring at the wall. *This is normal.*

And then, there's *another* way guys in puberty get erections—by thinking sexual thoughts. This usually only happens when you've gone through puberty and then start to have thoughts you've never had before. These thoughts are *totally* normal, and pretty much everyone has them. Sexual thoughts can cause erections even when you don't touch your penis. To most guys, touching their penises *feels pretty good.* After puberty, this touching can eventually result in ejaculation, or when the semen loaded with sperm comes out the end of your penis (see page 41). When this happens to a guy while he's sleeping, we call it a wet dream (see page 42), which is a natural thing that happens occasionally during puberty to almost all guys. When the guy is awake, we call it masturbation (see page 44).

. . . .

How do you control HARD-ONS?

Sometimes erections can happen at awkward times (like when you're asked to stand in front of the class or when you're walking down the hallway). There's not much to do except *wait for it to go down,* though some boys will turn away for a minute or try to think of something else (not sexual things). When you get older, you'll automatically learn to have more control over them. By the way, boys have lots of words—slang words like "hard-on"—for erections. You'll hear other boys use these words, and you might use them yourself. That's OK, as long as you know the real word too.

A question I have is, can you have an erection if you have to pee?

Guys sometimes get concerned about things getting **mixed up** down there. The good news is that your body is designed so that doesn't happen. When a guy has an erection, *he can't pee*. And when he's urinating, there will be **no surprise** erections. Clever, huh?

. . . .

Every time you get an erection, does SEMEN come out?

No, guys have plenty of erections that come and go without anything more happening. But keep reading further about **semen** and when it comes out.

. . . .

Is it hard to be social when having an ERECT PENIS?

It certainly could be! The thing is, depending on the type of pants you're wearing, most other people **can't tell**, even if *you* know you're having one. Then again, it could be *really difficult* to dance with one, or to have a serious conversation with your grandparents while having one!

9. If You Never Have Sex, Will **Your Balls** Just Keep Getting Bigger and Bigger?

. . . And Other Questions About Testicles, Sperm, and Related Things

What's in the testicle?

A **testicle** (also known as a *testis* or a *ball*) is a gland that makes testosterone, the hormone that makes us taller, stronger, hairier, and smellier. It also makes **sperm**. Sperm are single cells that, when combined with an egg from a woman, make a new person. When your testicles get the *hormone message* from the pituitary (that gland near your brain) telling them that puberty is starting, they start pumping out lots of **testosterone**, and at the same time, they make lots of sperm. Each day, a guy's testicles can make *millions of sperm*. Sperm get stored for a couple of days and then if you don't use them, your body destroys them and makes brand-new ones.

Are sperm actually ALIVE and do they know where to go?

Sperm are definitely alive, and they are some of the few cells in our bodies that can move around on their own. Sperm have tails and look like tadpoles. They also swim like tadpoles by shaking their tails back and forth. But they *don't have eyes and they don't have brains*, so they don't know where to swim—they just swim. If sperm are going to be used—like in wet dreams (see page 42), masturbation (see page 44), or sexual intercourse (see page 68)—they swim up two tubes, each called a vas, which bring them from the testicles to the urethra so they can come out the *end of the penis.*

. . . .

Does one testicle make one type of sperm and the other makes the other?

Most of us do have two testicles, and you're right—there are two types of sperm. Half of your sperm will have an X chromosome and would produce a *baby girl*; the other half have a Y chromosome in order to make a *baby boy*. Both testicles make both kinds. For more on that, see the chapter on pregnancy starting on page 83.

. . . .

If you never have sex, will your balls just keep getting bigger and bigger?

No! A guy would look pretty silly having testicles *the size of beach balls*! Testicles are little factories—their job is to make testosterone and sperm. To do their job, they do start growing when you begin puberty, but when they get to adult size at the end of puberty, that's it.

If you get hit in the testes, will you get damaged?

Most boys at some point get **accidentally** hit or kicked in their testicles—and they learn really quickly not to let that happen ever again! Boys have a lot of special **nerve** endings around their testicles reminding them to *protect them* and not let them get hit. If a boy does get hit, usually it just **hurts** a lot but gets better on its own. If it's a major hit, though, the testicle could be damaged. If a boy loses one testicle—by getting hit like that or having a disease like cancer—or if he was only born with one, that's OK. One **testicle** can do the job of two if it has to.

. . . .

What does it mean when balls (or testes) drop?

This may be a real *surprise*, but our testicles start out deep inside our *bellies*, not in the **scrotum**, or **sac**. Just a few weeks before we're born, our testicles *move down* through our groins and pop into our scrotums, where they should be when we're born. (Occasionally a testicle will get stuck along the way, and it needs to be helped along with surgery, or removed if it gets stuck deep inside.) The reason we have our testicles outside our bodies instead of deep inside where they could be protected is that they need to be a little **cooler** than our bodies in order to **make sperm.** As a guy moves through puberty, his testicles grow to their full size and *hang at the bottom of the scrotum*, therefore appearing to "drop." Once your testicles get into your scrotum, they can still move around a little. If they're too cold (like if you're standing in the ocean in the winter), the testicles will rise up as high as they can in the scrotum in order to get **warmer.** On the other hand, if they're too warm (like if you're really hot in the middle of summer), the testicles can *hang really low* in the scrotum to try to get *as cool as possible*.

What if one testicle grows bigger than the other?

Occasionally, one testicle can be slightly **bigger** than the other, and in almost all guys, the left testicle hangs **lower** than the right one. But, rarely, a guy can get a problem on his testicles or in his scrotum, so we tell all guys to *gently feel their testicles* every so often to make sure they're all right. There are several reasons a guy could feel something not right there—and the scariest thing would be cancer—but this is extremely rare and could be fully cured if found early enough. That's where you come in—you should **check regularly** to make sure your testicles are OK. *At your next physical exam*, you can ask your healthcare provider to talk with you about that.

. . . .

I have a lump in my nipple. Does that mean I have breast cancer?

First of all, **don't worry**—this isn't cancer and you're not developing female breasts. Remember all that **testosterone** that you start making in puberty that makes you taller, stronger, smellier, and hairier? Well, as it turns out, all guys in the world make both male hormones (like testosterone) and female hormones (like estrogen). What makes us *guys* is that we make a whole lot more male hormone than female. But when we're in puberty, our body is pumping out more of all these **hormones**, so we might produce a little more of the teensy amount of female hormones than ordinarily. About half of all guys see a little enlargement of one breast or both. Usually, it just feels like a **lump** under the nipple, but sometimes it could be a little larger. In almost all guys, *this goes away by itself* when puberty is over.

BLADDER
Pee Stored Here

URETHRA
Pee & Sperm Freeway

PROSTATE
Sperm's Little Helper

VAS DEFERENS
Sperm Highway

EPIDIDYMIS
Transportation & storage units

PENIS
You've Seen This Before

TESTICLES
Testosterone & Sperm Factories

SCROTUM
Testicle Sac

CIRCUMCISED PENIS

UNCIRCUMCISED PENIS

ERECT PENIS

What does the semen do? I only got info on the sperm.

The sperm is really, **really tiny**—you can't even see one without a microscope. It's also a *great swimmer* and goes fast considering its small size. But it has no reserve of energy, so it would run out if it didn't get a boost from something along the way. Sperm gets its *energy boost* from **semen**. Semen is a special liquid made by a gland called a **prostate** (and nearby structures called seminal vesicles). It keeps the sperm moist and provides sugars and other nutrients to give them the **energy** to *stay alive and finish their trip*. You can't see sperm, but you can see semen; it's white, and it looks like mucus.

Why do I hear my grandfather complain about the prostrate?

He's probably complaining about the **prostate**! That's an important gland for making the **semen** that nourishes the sperm. As a guy gets older, his prostate can have a harder time doing its job, so it might get larger to produce the same amount of semen. This could wind up pressing on his urethra, the tube that takes urine from the bladder to the penis, making it *harder for him to pee* (see the picture on the opposite page so this makes sense). This is why young boys can often pee farther and stronger than their dads and grandfathers.

. . . .

How does the sperm come out of the penis? Does it pee out or does it automatically come out?

When sperm are going to be used (during *wet dreams, masturbation,* or *sex*—see Chapter 10 and Chapter 14 for more on those), your **internal muscles** help them get up to the **prostate** to get surrounded by semen, then continue to help them along to the end of your penis, using the same route urine would take (but semen is different than urine!). Urine and semen with sperm never mix—only one can take that route at a time. When sperm and semen do come out (when your penis is erect), we call that **ejaculation**. It happens in a few spurts—maybe *a teaspoon total*—then it's over, and the penis goes back to its normal shape.

. . . .

What are JOCK STRAPS for?

When guys play certain sports, they wear *jock straps* under their shorts in order to **protect** their testicles. Jock straps not only keep the testicles closely tucked in so they won't get easily hit, they also make it more **comfortable** to run. Jiggling testicles can be a real annoyance!

10. I Don't Remember **Dreaming**. Am I Still Going to Enter Puberty?

. . . And Other Questions About Wet Dreams and Masturbation

What is a WET DREAM?
Is it really due to a dream?

After puberty begins, a boy's reproductive system does something I like to call *"testing things out."* Now that he is making testosterone and sperm, the system tries it out, at night, when he's asleep—in fact, when he's dreaming. Guys get erections when they dream (no matter what they're dreaming about). During a wet dream, the sperm come up from the testicles, join together with the semen, and come out the end of the penis together. Some guys might sleep through the whole thing and find a dried spot on their pajamas or sheets or underwear. It might look like they've peed in bed, but it's nothing like that. Other guys might wake up right after it happens and discover it: "Wow! What's that? Oh yeah, *it's that wet dream thing.*" It's totally normal and part of a guy growing up.

I don't remember dreaming. Am I still going to enter puberty?

You bet. A lot of people **can't remember** their dreams. That's OK—you're still dreaming even if you don't remember it, and that's when a **wet dream** happens. And not every guy remembers having a wet dream—that's OK too. *You'll still enter puberty at the normal time.*

Am I going to do this every night for the rest of my life?

Absolutely not. Some guys experience only **a couple** of wet dreams, while others have **a bunch** during puberty. Adult guys can occasionally get one, but not often. Somehow, once you get older, your body doesn't need to do this anymore.

. . . .

A boy at school says wet dreams are bad and he'd never had one.

Wet dreams are not bad—they're **normal**. Almost all grown-up men can remember having them. *It is just part of being a guy.* Does every guy have them? Well, some guys can't remember having one, but maybe they slept right through it and never noticed. That's OK too.

. . . .

What does it mean to "JACK OFF"?

"Jack off" is a slang term for **masturbation**. People use a lot of slang words for anything to do with sexuality. Why? Maybe because people *don't often talk about these things* or because some people say you shouldn't talk about them. When people are told not to talk about things, they often come up with other terms to say the same thing. Some of these are funny, but some, especially when kids use slang words for parts of other kids' bodies, can be disrespectful and hurtful. Is it OK to use **slang words** occasionally? That depends on who you're talking to, but remember that some people might not find them funny. Oh, and *be sure you know the real word* for things before you use the slang word.

Now back to masturbation. This is when a guy **touches** or rubs his penis until it becomes **erect** and then keeps rubbing it until he ejaculates (when the sperm come out in the semen). It's not something that happens by itself—it's something he chooses to do. Guys do this mostly because it **feels good**, though other guys

say it's a way of *working out their sexual feelings*. After a guy ejaculates, his penis returns to its relaxed state. And girls can masturbate too, but it's a bit different (see below and page 80 on the girls' side to learn more).

. . . .

Is there such a thing as TOO MUCH masturbation?

First of all, masturbation is a **choice** people make. Can a person choose not to do it? Sure. But the overwhelming majority of people do choose to masturbate at some point in their lives. Why? Because it **feels good**. You might wonder why, if it feels so good, guys don't masturbate a thousand times a day. Well, first, because they can't. It takes **body energy** to ejaculate and you just can't do it that often. The body needs time to *recharge energy* and *sperm*. More importantly, there are many other things you need to get done during the day—eating, sleeping, going to school, playing, and spending time with family and friends. Another very important issue is that in some families, some communities, and some faiths, **masturbation** is not felt to be an acceptable thing to do. Your parents and the other adults in your life may have some definite feelings and thoughts about this—so, *as awkward as it might be*, you could consider having a conversation with them about this.

. . . .

If you masturbate before puberty, will your dong be smaller?

If a guy rubs his penis before puberty, he might get an erection but probably won't ejaculate since sperm isn't being made yet. But certainly, it **won't** make your penis **smaller**, or do *anything else bad to you*. In order to persuade boys not to touch their penises, some adults make up things that could happen to you if you masturbate. *No*, masturbating won't make you crazy. *No*, masturbating won't make you go blind. *No*, masturbating won't give you more pimples or make you grow hair on your palms. And it definitely *won't* make your penis fall off! **Nothing bad** happens to your body if you masturbate, and you can't tell by looking at someone if they've ever done it.

11. Do Girls Fart?

... And Other Questions Boys Have About Girls and Their Bodies

Do girls get the same information about all this stuff as we do?

Hopefully! Of course, girls might have **different** questions than boys do, and be interested in slightly different things than boys are. You can read through the girls' section of this book to see what's different and what's the same.

. . . .

Do girls going through puberty realize that boys are changing also?

They sure do. Of course, it's OK to tell them what you're feeling during all these changes—just so they know your view of things. But when people are changing so fast in puberty and just learning how to manage their new **bodies**, they tend to focus on **themselves** a lot. We all need to pay some attention to *what's happening to others around us* too.

How come girls' hair is longer?

Because they **wear it** that way! It depends on the **culture** you're in and what's popular at the time, but in our culture, girls tend to wear their hair longer than boys do. However, *there are plenty* of boys who prefer to wear their hair longer and plenty of girls who like to have **shorter** hair.

. . . .

How come some girls have hair like a mustache?

All girls have some male-type **hormones** in their bodies—they make these hormones in various glands around their body. These are the hormones that help them grow taller, grow hair, and also contribute to body odor and pimples. Some women do grow just **a little hair** above their lips as a result (but *usually won't grow a beard*). And remember, the amount and type of hair we grow is determined by what we inherit from our birth families, so some girls might come from families where girls have more hair than others and some might come from those with less.

. . . .

Is it possible to be a boy and a girl? If so, what would happen when you go through puberty?

Almost all people tend to have one or the other complete set of **reproductive parts**, and it is rare for a baby to be born with both male and female sets or parts of each. Whichever set a person has tends to determine how puberty is going to happen. So a person with **boy** reproductive parts will produce testosterone, make sperm, get erections, and all that stuff we talked about; a person with **girl** reproductive parts will mature eggs in the ovaries, have periods, and all the rest. In the unusual situation that a baby's reproductive system is *different from one of these* sets, what happens in puberty will depend on the exact reason for their being different, so there isn't just one answer to this question because it's *more complicated*.

Can girls hold their pee?

Of course. Girls have **bladders** *just like boys do*. The bladder is a hollow muscle shaped like a ball. It fills with urine as the kidneys make it, stretching to hold as much as it can. When it gets full, you *empty your bladder* by letting the urine flow out the urethra (that hole at the end of your penis). Girls have a urethra too, only much shorter than yours since they don't have a penis. Because women are generally somewhat **smaller** than men, they might have slightly smaller bladders and therefore can't hold as much pee.

How do girls pee? Do girls pee out of their butt?

You might have noticed that guys can either sit down or **stand up** to pee, but girls have to **sit down**. Though guys can point their penis in the right direction when they pee (hopefully!), girls don't have penises, so their pee can really only go straight down. That's why they always need to sit when peeing. Guys have two openings in the pubic/butt area: the **urethra** at the end of their penis for both urine and semen (at different times, of course) and the anus for moving their bowels. Girls have three: the *urethra* for urinating; the **vagina** for having periods, sexual, intercourse, and birthing babies; and the *anus* for moving their bowels (see the picture on page 37 on the girls' side).

Why do girls go to the bathroom in groups?

Some girls enjoy being together and **sharing** their feelings and thoughts. Walking to the bathroom together can be another opportunity to socialize in small groups at school during breaks in the day.

Are girls circumcised?

Girls are **not circumcised**. In certain cultures, such as in parts of Africa, there is a custom called "female circumcision," but it's *not* circumcision and most of the rest of the world considers this *destructive* and **extremely hurtful** to the girls and is trying to eliminate this practice.

. . . .

Do GIRLS FART?

Everyone farts. It's possible you might not have noticed since girls might try harder than boys *not to do it in front of other people*. Girls burp too, by the way, and have stomach noises, just like us. There are more things that are the **same** about girls' and boys' bodies than are different, as it turns out.

. . . .

Why do girls have boobs but boys don't?

Biologically, females have breasts that can provide milk when it's time to **feed a baby**. Boys don't give birth to babies, nor do they have much estrogen to make breasts like women do. We do have nipples, however, which are left over from evolution. Sometimes boys' breasts can temporarily get bigger during puberty (see page 39). For many females, having breasts can also be an important part of being a **woman**. Oh, and as for using **slang** words for parts of the body—*be careful*. Though you might hear other people referring to breasts with slang words, many people find it disrespectful.

Do girls have anything similar to erections?

Well, *sort of.* In front of their urethral openings (where they pee from), women have a **clitoris** (see page 37 on the girls' side). About the size of a small pea, the clitoris can get slightly bigger when a woman gets sexually **excited**—just like a guy's penis. And like a penis, the clitoris is **sensitive** to touch. What this means is that, just like your penis, if touched gently, *it can feel good,* but if touched roughly, it can be really uncomfortable!

. . . .

When girls masturbate, what comes out? How do girls masturbate?

Girls can do something similar, although they don't have a penis to rub. Instead, they have a **clitoris**, a small structure near the outside of the vagina. When rubbed, this can give them a **good feeling** too. But *they don't ejaculate* since they don't make sperm or semen, and masturbating has no effect on their eggs. Girls don't report masturbating as much as boys do, but they can do it too. (See what girls say about masturbating on page 80 on the girls' side.)

. . . .

How do you know when a woman is having a period?

Mostly, *there is no way for you to know* unless she tells you. To learn exactly what a period is and more about them, check out Chapter 7 on the other side (since girls have *plenty* of questions about that themselves).

Does it hurt to put a tampon in or the boy equivalent?

A **tampon** is used by some girls during their periods to protect their clothes. A tampon is inserted into a girl's **vagina**, which is flexible and adapts to it. To learn more about periods, tampons, and vaginas, check out Chapter 7 on the girls' side. By "the boy equivalent" I imagine you are asking about when a penis is put into a vagina during sexual intercourse—again, a vagina *is adaptable* to a penis as well and it usually does not hurt. For more on sexual intercourse, keep reading.

. . . .

Do boys have periods like girls?

To have a period, a person has to have a **uterus**, the purpose of which is to have a **baby**. If you are not born with a uterus, you *can't have a period* (see Chapter 7 on the girls' side for more on this).

. . . .

Why do girls always want to be so clean?

Girls differ from boys in many ways, but remember that not all girls are the same, just like not all boys are the same. Besides their **genetic** and body **differences**, boys and girls are also frequently raised differently. Depending on the culture and the family, boys are encouraged to do certain things and act certain ways, while girls might be *encouraged differently*. Keeping things in order and clean could be one of those things. Again, there are certainly girls who are **messy** and certainly boys who are quite **neat**. Oh, and while you think of them as too clean, they might be thinking of you as too dirty or disorderly! It's all a matter of the way you look at people.

How do girls get to be so sexy?

Sexy is in the *eye of the beholder*! What is sexy for one person might not be for another. Maybe someone becomes **attractive** to you when they start to look grown-up or they change the way they look, or because you realize you feel good or special when you're around them. Or maybe you are finding another person attractive because you are **changing** yourself. (Remember that hormones are changing our brains too, and cause us to have new thoughts—thoughts of attraction. See page 55.) Actually, it's probably a *combination of things*!

. . . .

Why are girls so chatty and strange?

Girls tend to be more **vocal** and **expressive** than boys, though there are certainly girls who aren't. There are also boys who can be quite chatty and outgoing! *Girls can be different from boys*—both in their bodies and in the way they act and think. So until you get to know them (which could take a while!), they might seem a bit strange. (Want to know what they think about boys? See Chapter 12 on the girls' side.)

Why do women get crabby?

We *all* get **crabby** sometimes—it can happen because we're frustrated, or we don't feel well, or we're uncomfortable, or for a lot of other reasons. People have different ways of expressing their feelings, but *feelings are important* to healthy relationships and healthy decision-making. Next time you see someone who is crabby, sad, mad, or frustrated, you might try to find out what they're feeling that caused them to appear that way.

Are girls smarter or do girls just have bigger brains?

Neither. Girls may traditionally be better at **thinking** in some ways, and boys may traditionally be better at thinking in other ways, but these are generalizations. Since girls enter puberty sooner than boys (about two years earlier) and tend to be more verbal than boys, it might seem like girls are smarter, but boys and girls are about equal. And our brains are basically the **same size**.

Do girls care as much as guys about the things we're talking about?

You bet! Just check out the girls' side of this book to see the types of questions *girls are asking*.

12. What Do You Do on a Date, Exactly?

. . . And Other Questions About Dating, Relationships, and Attractions

When do boys start to have SEXUAL thoughts and is it sudden?

All boys (*and girls too*) will have sexual thoughts as they grow up—this is part of being a healthy human being and is *not bad or wrong*. It's normal. Although some people could begin having attractions earlier, most experience these near the start of puberty. It won't be something you wake up suddenly having—they come gradually. When people start to feel attractions, they start to notice other people more and notice different things about them than they used to. They might notice their faces, their body shapes, the way they move, or how they talk. You may find that you're seeing this in real people who pass by or in pictures of people in magazines. It might be that a person in your class who you didn't notice before is more interesting to you now. It could be that you notice different things about people's pictures in magazines or on television. Eventually, kids growing up "get it" that *these are thoughts of attraction* and are totally OK.

When do SEXUAL FEELINGS stop?

Usually, sexual feelings are *with you forever*. They can change, however, as you get older. Our thoughts and attitudes change, other people change, and we gain more experience by meeting new people. Let's just say those sexual feelings **will be there**, but perhaps they'll be different than they are now.

. . . .

Is it OK to have a girl as a friend?

You bet. You can be friendly with girls in your school, you can play sports or do activities with them, or you can just hang around with them like you would any guy friend. Some people (like your guy friends) might wonder if there's something romantic going on, but that might be because they don't have any girls as friends themselves and don't know that it's possible to be *friends with girls*. Just to be sure, you can even talk it over with the girl and say you **like her as a friend** and ask how she'd feel having a guy as a friend. Most adults have friends of the opposite gender, so it's a **pretty normal thing**. There are some cultures where this is not a usual thing, so you can also *ask your family* about this subject.

. . . .

How do you TALK TO A GIRL without flirting with them?

As a person gets *more experience* in dealing with **attractions**, they learn ways to show their attraction, which some call flirting. They also learn how to **interact** with others without flirting (like with their cousin or the person who works at the grocery store or the babysitter). This mostly comes from trial and error, but you can get some clues from *watching how other people* around you (like ones in your family or other grown-ups) do it. **Flirting** means using your words and behaviors to

show you are interested and attracted to someone beyond a regular conversation or friendship—like with jokes, eye contact, or physical closeness. The person flirting needs to pay attention to the other person's response—if the other person is not interested in the attention, the flirting *needs to stop*.

What do you do on a date, exactly?

Dates can be **different** things for different people, but most think of them as a way to get to know someone in whom you're **interested**. It could be going to a dance, to the mall, or to a movie, or just *hanging out and talking*. Most families have important **rules** for dating—this is because they want to make sure you feel safe while being able to have a good time. Some rules might be that your parents need to know who you're with, where you're going, and when you're coming home. Although some teens might think their parents are being too protective or strict, a lot of teens are also happy their parents *care enough to keep them safe*.

How old do I have to be to start dating?

Well, there's no set rule on that, except that it's the age your **family** feels comfortable with. Sometimes boys start with a **group date**—several boys and girls doing some **activity** together—before considering the type of date with just two people. Again, your family wants you to be safe, so they might want you to *wait until they know you will be*. Some families come from cultures where dating is not done at all, and kids only get to know each other at family events. Other families come from cultures where dating is OK. Try *asking the grown-ups in your life* what rules about **dating** they had when they were teenagers.

I have never gotten a date—will I ever?

If you're ten, eleven, twelve, or even fifteen, that's **normal**. People sometimes wait until **later** to date because they're not *ready* or because their families *aren't comfortable* with dating yet. Don't worry—there will be lots of **time** and lots of **opportunities** to date.

What is the best way to ask them out that has the best chance of "yes"?

You probably already know the answer to that one. *We all like people* who are **kind**, considerate, and **friendly**—the same sort of things you would like in a friend of yours. Since almost all adults have *a whole bunch of experience* with this sort of thing, it might be fun to ask them what worked for them and what didn't. This type of **challenge** hasn't changed at all since they were dating, so perhaps you could learn from what they learned.

. . . .

What do you do if they say no?

This can happen. **Rejection** is part of *the growing-up experience*. Though sometimes it can make you feel bad, having someone say no will help you **learn** something that makes you better at asking the next time. And remember, someone might ask you out and you have the same option of saying no if that person *isn't right for you*. The important thing to know is that there are people out there who will say yes when you ask them, who will want to spend time with you and get to know you, and who will be fun to hang out with.

. . . .

What should you say if a really hot girl asks you out?

First, be careful with terms like "hot" to describe others, since that usually means "sexy," or someone seen only as a sexual object, and doesn't describe all the other good things about that person, such as their friendliness, charm, or how funny or clever they can be. Although in the old days guys almost always did the asking, these days *anyone* can ask *anyone* out. If this happens, you get to **decide** if you want to go out. *Are you ready?* It can take some effort to figure this out. Most people say that

it's not just how attractive the other person is, but a lot of different factors that help you decide. Do you have things in **common**? Is this person **fun** to be with? Do you know the person enough to be able to make a decision? You can ask other people who have gone on dates (like your parent or some other trusted adult) for *tips on what to do and how to manage things* if someone asks you out. Or you can just say yes, realizing that sometimes dates are really great and mostly a *learning experience*.

How do you get a girlfriend?

Let's start with what a **girlfriend** is. Sometimes, guys can call a friend who is a girl a "girl friend." But usually, when guys use that word, it means someone you're dating **exclusively**—that means you're dating that girl *and no one else*. (Some families will be OK with you dating, but would prefer you to not go **steady** yet—that means not be with just one person all the time.) Then, if you're ready and your family's OK with it, you still have to *find someone*! If you're **friendly**, have a sense of **humor**, are considerate and a **good listener**—and if you can be yourself—it would be hard for girls *not* to like you!

Is love meant to just keep us reproducing?

There are plenty of people who **fall in love** with another person and never have children together. Falling in love happens when someone becomes totally **attracted** to another person and wants to be with them *as much as possible*. Sometimes that leads to **marriage**, but not always. Sometimes those couples decide to have children, *but not always*. Think about a couple who meets when they're your grandparents' age—they can fall in love just like younger people, but they might not be thinking about having kids.

I don't want to kiss. What do I do?

Sounds like you're **not ready**, which is *just fine*. Of course, if Aunt Tillie wants to give you a kiss on the cheek, you might have to deal with that. But **romantic** kissing is something people choose to do with someone they are attracted to. There are still plenty of other things you can do to show you like someone: **smile** at them, **laugh** with them, *say nice things* to them, do fun things with them—these are just a few but there are many, many more.

. . . .

Is it normal to kiss a girl when you're eleven years old? Will it hurt you?

Some kids can **feel attraction** earlier than other kids. And you might have seen a romantic kiss in a movie and wondered what it's like. No, it won't hurt you, but be sure that it's OK with the person you're kissing! Also, **touching** someone like this gives them the signal that you're attracted to them. If you're not, maybe you'd better hold those kisses for someone *you are attracted to*.

. . . .

Why do girls bother, trick, and spy on boys?

Girls generally enter puberty before boys do and progress through it **a little faster**. So while boys might still be interested mostly in themselves, girls might be curious or interested in what boys are thinking and doing, and want to *be around them* to find out.

What are the chances that two people will be attracted to each other? How does it happen?

If *falling in love* was like it is in the movies, you'd think it's like **magic**. It can happen that way in real life, but a lot of the time it takes people a while to realize they might be in love with, or even **attracted to**, another person. With all the people on this earth, you can bet there is someone out there who will be as attracted to you as you will be to them—and my bet is that there is more than just one. The **fun** is in *finding the person who is right for you.*

. . . .

Do I have to get married?

Most people find that as they grow up, they really want to be with another person and get **very close** to that person. In many families, cultures, and communities, that might mean getting **married**. Hold off on that thought for now—*you're just beginning to grow up*. Lots of **changes** await you, and you might find that what you want changes too. Getting married is a choice for most people in this country—you can ask people around you who are married why they chose marriage. Then, when you're old enough, you can **decide** *if you want to get married or not.* In some countries and in some cultures, marriage is something your parents may decide for you—if you come from one of these cultures, you'll need to talk with your parents about it.

What's it like to fall in love?

There's a ton of music, poetry, movies, and books written about that! Love makes some people feel like they're going a little **crazy**, with all their thoughts focused on that other person. They can even stop doing things they've always liked to do. Some people describe love as *a terrific feeling* that **overwhelms** them. And some people just **wonder** if the feelings they have inside must be love, though they aren't sure. Love can be very different for different people. Try asking the adults in your life *how love feels to them*.

When a guy and a girl have a relationship does the guy have to be older?

No, but because girls **mature** a little sooner than boys, and if a boy and girl are dating, you sometimes see girls with boys who are the same age or maybe a year or two older if they are in high school. When you're an adult, age matters less. What is really important, though, is to have **things in common** to talk about, and you should have about the same level of experience with someone you are dating. Healthy relationships are strongest when two people share things equally, which includes similar life stories and experiences. If one person is an adult and the other is still a kid, however, there are laws throughout the country that protect the young person so that they are not taken advantage of by the older person.

Why do some humans act homosexually?

Homosexual (or *gay*) is the word for someone who is sexually attracted to someone of his or her own gender. Most people are *heterosexual* (or *straight*), which means they are sexually attracted to the other gender. As far as we know, there have been **gay people** in every culture on earth for as long as humans have existed. One way to think about people being gay or straight is to think about people being

left-handed or right-handed. Most people are right-handed, but that doesn't mean that being left-handed is wrong or bad. Does someone choose to be left-handed? *No, they were born that way.* Can you tell if someone is left-handed when they're born? No, you have to wait until they grow up enough to use one hand more than the other. Human **sexuality** is probably similar, but much more **complicated**. People don't choose to be sexually attracted to others of the same gender—they just *discover it when it happens.*

Some people who are gay act **different** than people who are straight. Other people who are gay act just like people who are straight. But you know what? Not all straight people act the same either. People can act more masculine or feminine, and it often has nothing to do with their sexual orientation. Being gay or straight has to do with the *person you are sexually attracted to,* not how you talk or walk or dress or act.

. . . .

When some guy is gay, is it because he gets too many of his genes from the mom (because mom likes boys so the gay guy likes boys)?

That's a very interesting thought! Scientists have tried to figure out why people are **straight** or **gay**. So far, all they know is that it has *nothing to do with hormones* (we know that gay males have the same amount of testosterone as straight males), the way they were parented, or anything else that has been suggested. Perhaps one day scientists will discover why a person is gay, but in the meantime, we consider this an example of *being different but normal.*

If I am gay should I mask it?

First, **sexual attractions** can be confusing and complicated. Some people question their attractions and what they mean. That's OK—it can take quite a while to figure this all out. But, if you do realize you are attracted to guys, or perhaps both guys and girls, then *you should not keep it to yourself,* because that could make you feel very **alone**. There are many people *who do not understand* being gay, and there are many people who feel it is bad—so it's natural to want to keep it to yourself so you don't get teased, or worse. But sexuality is part of every person on earth, and it's important to recognize **who you are** and talk with someone about it. Sometimes talking with your parents is a good place to start, since they are the ones who care most about you. Because a lot of cultures, religions, communities, and families have **strong opinions** about sexual orientation, this could be a very hard subject for them to talk about. If you feel like you can't talk to your parents, maybe you can identify another trusted adult, such as a teacher or other relative, to confide in. There are also good **resources** online and books about sexuality to help you out. The important thing to remember is that *you are not alone,* and you are a **normal** and **valued** person, just like everyone else.

. . . .

What should I do if someone is calling me gay?

People sometimes call other people names just to **tease** them. They make fun of the way you look or what you wear or how you talk. They might do that to impress their friends or because they think it's funny. These people are **bullies** (the same stuff happens to girls; see page 54 on the girls' side). If you're being teased or bullied, that is not OK—and you should let an adult know who can help you stop it or help you learn ways to deal with it.

Can two people of the same sex get married?

It's now **legal** throughout the United States and in many other countries for men to marry men and women to marry women. *Any two people* who are adults, who **love** each other, and who want to remain together for all time can express that by getting married to each other. Some people choose to never marry—it's a *big decision* to dedicate yourself to another person in this way, so different people make all kinds of different choices.

What I Wish Other People Knew About Me

- I just want to be nice
- I am sensitive about stuff they say and I try to hide it with a smile; for example, when some of my friends say, "you suck" or something, I hide it with a smile
- I'm not like my brother, and I hate it when people compare me to him
- That I try to stand up to people and not do everything that the popular kids do
- I can act mature—I just don't like to a lot
- That I am not a good athlete
- I want to learn a lot and be smart but also be popular at the same time
- I don't like sports
- That everyone has a different talent
- I have feelings
- I need a little space sometimes

13. Can **Sex** Happen Accidentally?

. . . And Other Questions About Sex and Sexually Transmitted Infections (STIs)

What is sex, exactly?

Sex is a small word that describes a whole lot of things. When most people talk about sex, they're talking about **sexual intercourse**. Let's say that a man and a woman are sexually attracted to each other. If the guy has sexual thoughts, his penis will get erect. Then he and the woman get very **close**, skin to skin actually, and he inserts his erect penis into her vagina. If he moves it back and forth, it's just like rubbing his penis. (Remember we talked about that? See page 44.) The rubbing calls on the sperm to move from his testicles, combine with semen, and shoot out the end of his penis (that's called ejaculation). He feels a *total-body sensation*, called an **orgasm**.

Of course, people who feel sexual can express those feelings with others in many ways, such as kissing and hugging, and can also be between people of the same gender. Keep reading for more info on this.

How was sex invented?

No one "invented" or "discovered" sex—sex has always been a part of life. In fact, *it's how we got here*. As animals evolved, new animals came into being from sexual interactions. Sex is the way we reproduce ourselves.

. . . .

What are some reasons people have sex? Tell me as many as you know.

People have sex to have babies. People have sex because it feels good. People have sex because it is one of the most powerful things two people can do to feel really intimate, or close to each other. There are also other reasons people have sex that might not be as good—for instance, some boys feel they need to have sex because they *think* all other boys are doing it and they don't want to be left out. We'll talk about that again later.

. . . .

When the penis goes into the vagina, is that literal?

Absolutely. The penis is basically designed for the vagina, and vice versa. If this is really surprising to you, join the club! It is for many boys when they first learn about it.

Although this is frequently what people refer to when they say sex, there are *many other ways* two people can be sexually close to each other.

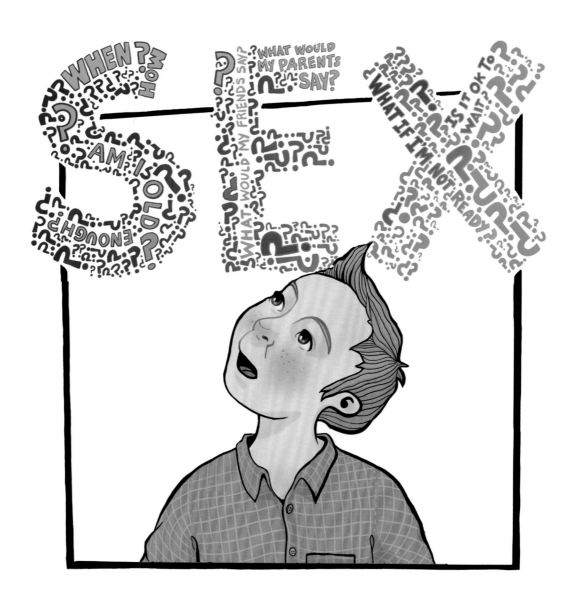

What if your penis doesn't fit in the vagina?

Lots of people, both boys and girls, worry about this. Don't worry—**it will**. But remember that to be a **respectful** partner, you should make sure you're not hurting the other person or doing something to make that person uncomfortable. And the other person should do the same for you.

. . . .

What does an orgasm feel like? PLEASE ANSWER!

It's hard to describe, but I'll try. An orgasm is a total-body sensation a person feels when at the height of sexual excitement. Your **heart** beats faster, your muscles get tighter, you sweat, you breathe faster, and it feels pretty good. Some guys say it feels like a **release**, some say it feels like an **explosion**, and some say *it just feels great*.

. . . .

What does a girl feel during sex?

Thanks for asking that question! Some guys only think about themselves when having sex and forget that they have a **partner** with whom they're having this *amazing experience*. Although a girl doesn't have a penis, she does have something called a **clitoris** located near the vagina that is similar—it's **sensitive** and it feels good when touched. Girls have orgasms too, but they sometimes need more **attention** and more time to experience one than a guy. That's why it's so important to talk about this stuff to learn how to be considerate of your partner. (Do you want to know more about what girls feel about sex? Flip over to Chapter 13 on the girls' side to find out.)

Do both of you (boy/girl) have to be naked when you have sex?

Well, that's generally the way it's done. There are many parts of our **bodies** that can feel good when **touched** romantically by another person, and *being naked* is the best way to make this happen. But you need at least to take clothes off the essential parts (*the penis* and *the vagina*) to engage in vaginal intercourse.

When do you have sex? How old? Where? When? Why?

Those are a lot of questions! Many young people wonder at what age people start having sex. There is an answer, but it's not a specific age—a person should have sex when they're **ready**. And ready means **different** things for different people. For some, it means waiting until a long-term committed relationship such as marriage. For others, it means when they understand how to prevent some of the things they don't want from sex, such as an unwanted pregnancy or a sexually transmitted infections. It doesn't make sense to just do what you think your friends are doing, since people tend to exaggerate about this stuff. When you're a teenager or young adult listening to others, you might think that you're the only one who hasn't had sex yet—*not true*. Lots of people wait because they feel they're not ready. The important thing to remember is that having sex is a **choice** you make, and only when you're ready. Oh, and don't forget your **partner** needs to feel ready too!

Is there a sign that tells you that you are READY to have sex?

Not that I can think of, except the **feeling** that you might be ready, and **knowing** that the other person is also ready. That's *equally important*.

. . . .

Will sex affect my daily life?

Some teens spend a lot of time **thinking** about sex. But there are a lot of other things to do as well—school, homework, sports, hobbies, spending time with family, eating, hanging out, etc. Make sure you leave **time** for all that other stuff—*sex will happen when you are ready*.

. . . .

What makes a man think that sex is disgusting when they are young but when they get older they like sex?

During puberty, your brain changes, just like your body. **Testosterone** causes new thoughts and **desires** to come your way, and as you grow up, you experience a ton of things that are new to you. A year from now, you could have *a totally different attitude* about something that you find gross now. Or it might take ten years for your opinions to change. That's OK—each guy takes his own time to get comfortable with all these changes.

Can you ACCIDENTALLY PEE in a girl's vagina when having sex?

The answer is, no! Because a vagina is a muscular canal made of soft tissue that connects to the uterus, it takes an erect penis to get inside—a relaxed penis just won't go in. When a penis is erect, it closes off the connection to the bladder so you can't pee. *Amazing* how it works that way. If you don't believe me, someday you can try to pee with a full erection—you really can't. And it works the other way too—when a penis is relaxed, you can't ejaculate semen. So you don't have to worry that semen and sperm will just come out at embarrassing times. **It all works out**.

. . . .

Can sex happen ACCIDENTALLY?

No. Sex is something one **chooses** to do. Sometimes when a guy does something that he later feels he shouldn't have, he might try to use the excuse that it was "accidental." But we all know it *doesn't work like that*.

. . . .

Why do people have sex if they don't want a baby?

People have sex because it **feels good** and because it makes them feel really **close** to each other in their relationship. But, since there's a chance sex between a man and a woman can result in getting pregnant, both partners have to understand this. If you and your partner are not ready to be parents, then *you both need to think ahead* to keep this from happening. (See page 93 on the girls' side for more information on preventing unwanted pregnancy.)

What do you do other than penis into vagina when you have sex?

Sex is a *little* word with a *lot* of meanings. You can **feel** sexual without *doing* anything. To some people, hugging and holding hands can be really sexual. Our **bodies** have lots of places that can make us feel sexual—experiencing sex with another person means **exploring** what's sexual for you and what's sexual for them. For a lot of boys, getting your first **romantic kiss** can give you a thrill down your spine—*that's being sexual too.*

. . . .

How do we figure out how to have sex?

Knowing how to have sex is part of **being ready**. You can read about it in a trusted book (like this one!), you can learn about it in school, you can talk with your parents about it, and you can learn from your sexual partner when you talk things through. But like any new **experience**, it can be a little nerve-racking when you're not sure what you're doing—that's *true for everyone*.

. . . .

My friend thinks that when you kiss the woman gets pregnant. Is that true?

No, just **kissing** can't possibly lead to pregnancy. A woman gets pregnant when a sperm gets to her egg. Her eggs are down in her **reproductive system** (see illustrations on page 37 on the girls' side), so that's where a guy's sperm has to go to get her **pregnant**. There have been many, many myths over the centuries about how someone gets pregnant. But now you *know how it really happens*, so when a friend comes up to you and says, "I heard a girl can get pregnant when a boy shakes her hand or winks at her," you can set him straight.

What does a date have to do with sex?

Some boys get confused and think a date is the same thing as having sex. *Not true*. A date is when two people **spend time** together. A date could be getting a snack at a restaurant, watching a movie, taking a walk together, or even just hanging out and talking. On the other hand, sometimes boys think a date is the right **opportunity** to have sex and may be hoping for it since they might be alone with the person they're dating. (See Chapter 12 for more on dating.)

. . . .

Why do people want to pretend to have sex?

Some people think it will **impress** others to tell them they've had sex because they think others will like them, respect them, or think they're cool. It's just like **bragging** in any other way—like telling others you've got superpowers or climbed Mount Everest blindfolded. Since *it's normal* to want to feel **important** and be included, someone might resort to bragging because they think it's the only way to get the positive attention they want. But weirdly, the more someone brags, the less others want to be around them. If someone announces that they've had sex, you might think of them as grown up, or you might think of them as foolish.

. . . .

How does it work from being boyfriend/girlfriend to sex?

Many, many couples decide to go steady but wait on having sex until they're **ready**. Also many families, faiths, cultures, and communities have fairly strong feelings about when people should have sex, or even go steady. Many teens decide that being ready is very important to them too, and hold off on having sex. In any case, it's not just you who has to be ready—it's **both** of you. You can do a million things with someone you care about—and show you really care about them—without having sex with them.

When people get married, do they have sex every day?

No, most married people don't have sex every day. Sex is a very special thing people share with each other—*it takes time and caring*. People have to work, sleep, eat, take care of the kids, and do other things they like to do. Sometimes it's hard to find time to fit sex in!

. . . .

What would I do if I was forced to have sex and I didn't want to?!

Sex should only happen if both people are ready and in agreement. If one person is not ready and the other person forces them to have sex, then it's seriously bad. It's not only hurtful and disrespectful, it's also illegal. Also if someone says no to sex and the other person tries to talk them into it until the other person just gives in, then that is forcing too. Some guys think that a girl is supposed to say no when first asked to have sex, even if she really wants to. But no means no. They don't need to give a reason why. Sometimes people are reluctant to say no because they don't want to seem mean or unfriendly, even if they are not ready. You actually have to hear a yes before you know they are really ready. And they could say yes but then change their mind and say no and then you stop and that's OK. So what can *you* do if someone is pressuring you to have sex and you're not ready? You could simply say no. If you like the person but you're not ready, you could say, "I'm just not ready for that, but we can still do other things together." Or, if the person is hurting you, or doesn't stop pressuring you when you already said no, you can *tell a trusted adult* or the authorities. *No one* should be forced to have sex if they are not ready.

What if I did not want to have sex and yet I want to have kids?

Well, you certainly could adopt children as an alternative to having them yourself. But wait on that decision until you're older. You might just *change your mind*.

. . . .

Why haven't I heard about what sex is before now?

It might be because you are now grown up enough to understand all this. It could also be because some grown-ups can feel awkward talking about sex if they've never talked about it with their kids before. Maybe *their* parents never spoke about it because it was awkward for them. It's just one of those topics that can feel embarrassing to talk about, plus there are *many* cultures, faith traditions, and families that discuss this subject in different ways. Parents and other trusted adults are a great place to learn about this, but there are also books and websites that the grown-ups in your life can show you. Some kids have classes on sex and health education in school. Some kids go to classes with their parent or other grown-ups so they can both learn at the same time.

. . . .

Do you have to do it?

You mean sex? No. Some people choose never to have sex, for various reasons. Sex is a choice—except when it is forced and then it's wrong. Most people in the world choose to have sex, however. Why? There are many reasons. To be *close to someone*, to experience it, and to be a parent are just a few.

What disease can you get from having sex that you can't die from?

Sometimes we can get diseases that make us **sick**. For example, you can get a cold if another kid with a cold coughs or sneezes in your direction. There are other diseases that can come from sexual contact with another person—these are called sexually transmitted diseases, or STDs. You'll also hear people refer to them as sexually transmitted infections, or **STIs**. There are a whole bunch of them. Some are caused by viruses, some by bacteria, and some by other things. Some STIs (like *chlamydia*) can be cured by taking **medicine**; some can be prevented by having a **vaccine** but not cured once you have them, like human papillomavirus (HPV); while others can be extremely serious and have **no cure**, like human immunodeficiency virus (HIV)—the virus that causes acquired immunodeficiency syndrome (AIDS). The only totally effective way—absolutely, without question—to avoid ever getting an STI is to never **have sex** with anyone. *Can you choose that*? Yes, you can. But as we discussed before, there would be some things you'd be missing out on, such as fathering a child of your own someday. So there are **precautions** you can take to avoid getting one of these infections—staying with one sexual partner, using condoms, getting a vaccine to prevent some STIs, getting you and your partner tested before having sex—but there is always some risk when one chooses to have sex.

. . . .

Do a lot of people have sex diseases? About how many?

Enough people have **STIs** that you need to think about it *before having sex*. You usually *can't tell* by looking at someone if they have an STI. Most of the infections aren't visible—meaning you may have one with no **symptoms**. Many people who have an STI have no idea that they have it. So how can you know? You can **get tested**—at your doctor's office or at a special clinic. Tests could include an exam

and perhaps a urine test or a blood test. Are the tests perfect? Well, not entirely, but they're really, really good at helping you know if you have an STI.

. . . .

What is AIDS? How do you get it? Did they have it when you were growing up?

Acquired immunodeficiency syndrome, or **AIDS**, is a disease caused by a virus called human immunodeficiency virus, or **HIV**. Like most viruses, HIV is **incurable**, though we've recently discovered some medicines that can mostly control it—but someone with HIV would have to take these drugs for the rest of their life. HIV damages your **immune system**, which protects you from infections and from cancers. So people with AIDS can get very sick and **die** from these things. When someone first gets HIV, they usually have no clue that the virus is working inside them—there are no particular symptoms—so the only way to know is to take a **test**. The test is easy and great at telling someone if they have HIV or not. Once the virus stays around for a while, it can progress to the disease AIDS, which can make a person **very sick**.

You can get HIV by having sexual contact with someone who has the **virus**, even if they don't seem sick at all. You can also get it by getting someone else's **blood** in your body, like through a blood transfusion. (Don't worry—the blood you would get in a hospital in the United States is checked completely and is extremely safe.) Also people who use certain **drugs** that require injection by needle, such as heroin, can get the virus by sharing someone else's needles.

Was AIDS around when we were growing up? Not that we knew of, but it probably came from another country where it only affected a few people. AIDS became big news when it spread to many people all over the world.

If you have a condo, can you still get HIV?

I think you mean a **condom**! A condom is made of latex or plastic, looks like a water balloon, and fits over a guy's erect penis before he has sex with someone. Guys use it to **prevent an STI** (either getting one or giving one) and to prevent female sexual partners from getting **pregnant**. You can buy condoms of all types at drugstores or convenience stores. To prevent STIs or pregnancy, a guy has to use one **every time** he has sex, not just occasionally, and put it on his erect penis before it gets close to his sexual partner. When he ejaculates (when sperm come out), the condom catches his sperm and semen, which prevents their contact with his sexual partner. *Does it work perfectly?* Well, it works really well for some diseases, like HIV, if used properly. For other diseases that can be elsewhere on your body other than your penis, such as crabs (little insects that can be anywhere on your skin), condoms aren't as effective. The biggest reason condoms might not work is that guys don't use them **properly**—it's totally OK to ask your parent or another trusted adult how to use a condom the right way (since the instructions are not on the condom wrapper).

. . . .

How does it feel to wear a condom?

It feels *like a tight piece of skin* over your penis. Most condoms are made so that guys still **feel everything** they would without one, but a guy might want to try different brands to see which works best for him. Some guys (and women!) have an allergy to the latex, so they make non-latex condoms too. You might hear guys tell you they don't like how the condom feels, but getting an STI or making someone pregnant *can feel a lot worse!*

How can a girl get pregnant and still prevent getting an STI?

Great question! You might be wondering how a couple that tries to prevent STIs (by having the guy use a condom) can *make a baby* if they want to. The simple answer is: you usually can't get **pregnant** if you use a condom—that same condom that keeps diseases from spreading also keeps the sperm from the egg. But there is a way to prevent STIs without preventing pregnancy—have sex with only **one partner**, who also has never had sex with anyone but you. That way, neither of you could have picked up an STI to give to the other. This is one reason why some people choose to wait to have sex until they are in a long-term **relationship**, such as marriage. Still another option is for each of you to *get tested for STIs* before having sex together. The tests aren't perfect, but they are really good at **preventing** STIs. Both people need to be sexual with that one person only, since once they have sex with someone else, there's the risk of getting an STI. It takes two people to think through how to avoid getting or passing STIs. And two people of the *same* gender can also get or pass an STI, depending on how sexual they are with each other.

But what if you don't want to make someone pregnant right now either? Are there other ways to keep from getting pregnant if a couple doesn't want it? Sure! Besides having the guy use a **condom**, you can choose not to have sexual intercourse, there are various hormones the woman can take, there's spermicide that kills sperm, there are **devices** a woman can use to block her cervix—and more. Go to page 93 on the girls' side to learn more about all that.

14. Is a **Pregnant** Man Possible?

. . . And Other Questions About Pregnancy and Childbirth

If you are a boy, and you're having sex with a girl, will the girl always have a baby?

So now that we've talked about sexual intercourse, let's talk about **pregnancy**. If a guy ejaculates when his penis is inside a woman's vagina, then millions of sperm are released inside her, right near her cervix, or the entrance to her uterus (see the picture on page 37 on the girls' side). Since **sperm** don't really know where to go, they will swim in all directions, but lots of them will happen to swim through a tiny hole in the cervix, through the uterus, and up into the fallopian tubes. If there's an egg already moving down one of these tubes, then the first sperm to get to the **egg** combines with it to *start a pregnancy*. If there is no egg in the tube at the time, then the sperm simply die and are eliminated by the woman's body.

Once a single sperm combines with an egg, the egg puts a wall around itself, which prevents any more sperm from getting in. In the meantime, the chromosomes from the egg (which come from the mom) and those from the sperm (which come from the dad) combine. Right away, the cells start multiplying as a *new baby* starts to form. This **zygote**, or combined egg and sperm, gets moved down to the uterus, where it sticks to the uterine wall, which has been preparing for it. And it **grows** and **grows**.

About **nine months** later, the baby is done growing and is ready to come out. He or she sends a message to the uterus (a strong muscle that stretches really big to hold the growing baby), which then contracts and pushes the baby down. The tiny hole in the cervix has to stretch to let the baby's head through, which usually comes first. *Ouch*! Both the contractions of the uterus and the stretching of the hole in the cervix hurt a lot—like a muscle cramp in your leg but much stronger. This is why they call it *labor pain*. Finally, a **baby** gets pushed out through the vagina and is born!

. . . .

I heard I was too big to be born the usual way. So how did that work?

Most babies are born through the **vagina**, with their heads coming through first. Some are turned around, with their butt coming first. Some babies can be **too big** to fit through, no matter how hard the mom is trying to push them out. In these cases, the doctor will anesthetize the mom (put her to sleep or numb her up) and make a **cut** down low in her belly, right into the uterus, and take the baby out that way. Then the mom gets sewn back up. This is called a cesarean section or **C-section**.

. . . .

What does it mean when my mom tells me she "tied the knot" so she won't have any more kids?

That means your mom asked a **surgeon** to cut her fallopian tubes (which carry the egg to the uterus and the sperm to the egg) and **tie off** the ends. Women can choose to do this to make sure they *never get pregnant* if they don't want any more babies. There are other ways to keep from getting pregnant—this is called **con-traception** or birth control (you can learn more on page 93 on the girls' side). If someone doesn't want to be pregnant, then both people in the relationship need to think about how to prevent it. Men can also "tie the knot" in this way. If they want to make sure no sperm come out that could make a woman pregnant when

they are having sexual intercourse, they could choose to have a **vasectomy**. This is something a doctor does in the office by making a small cut in the man's scrotum, finding the vas deferens that carry the sperm up from the testicles, and tying them off so *no sperm get through*. He can still have sex normally and will still produce semen but there will be no sperm in it to risk a pregnancy.

. . . .

Is a boy's birth different from a girl's?

No, they are exactly the **same**.

. . . .

When a sperm and an egg meet and make a baby, is it the first time it works or do you do it many times?

Since a woman's **egg** ripens *only once a month* and a baby can only start in the fallopian tube, there is really only about one week out of every month when a woman can get **pregnant**. If a woman has sex during this week then she could get pregnant, but some couples have to have sex **several times** before the woman gets pregnant. If a couple has sex at other times when there isn't an egg in the tube, then the woman won't get pregnant. Also, because some women don't know exactly when the egg is going to start its trip into the fallopian tube, relying on just not having sex during that fertile week is not a dependable way to prevent pregnancy.

Can a woman give birth without having sex?

Generally speaking, a woman can't give birth without having sex, since *having sex is the main way of getting pregnant*. A woman might choose to get donated sperm inserted into her vagina in a doctor's office or clinic—this is called artificial insemination. Also, in modern times, scientists have discovered that it's possible for doctors to remove an egg surgically from the woman's ovary, get some sperm from the man, and combine them in the laboratory. Then this zygote, or combination of egg and sperm, is placed back into the woman's uterus to grow into a baby. This process is called in vitro fertilization or IVF, and some couples might choose to do this if they are *having trouble* getting pregnant the traditional way.

. . . .

How do girls know that they're pregnant?

Some women know that they're pregnant as soon as their periods stop happening (see Chapter 7 on the girls' side for lots more details about periods). Women *don't* have bleeding, or periods, when they're pregnant because the uterus is holding on to its lining to start growing the baby. When a woman is pregnant, she can also have other symptoms that come from the pregnancy hormones her body makes—symptoms like an upset stomach or a different appetite. Also most women notice their bellies grow as the uterus gets larger. But if it's *really early* in the pregnancy, a woman may do a simple urine test that can tell her she's pregnant even before she feels anything.

Can a baby come out the butt?

No, never. Babies are born through a woman's **vagina**, which is a different area (see the picture on page 37 on the girls' side). For more on how the girl's reproductive system works, see Chapter 7 on the girls' side.

. . . .

If a guy has masturbated in a public toilet and doesn't flush it, and then a girl drops an egg in the toilet, and the sperm is still alive, will a baby grow in the toilet?

Sperm need special conditions to stay alive—they need to be kept moist and close to body temperature. If sperm left your body and ended up on a toilet seat, they'd **die** pretty quickly. And eggs can generally only get fertilized when they're in the fallopian tube (except in the case of in vitro fertilization; see the opposite page for more about this). So by the time an egg passes through a woman's vagina, it's **too late** for it to get fertilized. Plus, a baby needs a **uterus** to develop and grow. So there are *lots of reasons* why this can't possibly happen!

. . . .

Would the size of a woman's egg affect the height of the child?

No, **eggs** are all the same size and look about the same. But inside, each one carries a slightly different set of the woman's **genes**. Each one brings a message about how tall a baby should be. Of course, so do men's **sperm**. Boys tend to take after their dads a little more than their moms, and guys tend to be taller than women, but *both the egg and the sperm* are important in determining exactly how tall a baby will grow to be.

Where does the umbilical cord come from?

Right after an egg and a sperm get together, the special lining of the uterus gives the growing baby what it needs for **nutrition**. But as the baby gets bigger, the uterine lining forms into a special organ called a *placenta*, which connects itself to the baby at its belly button through a long cord-like thing, which is called the **umbilical cord**. The umbilical cord *carries food and oxygen* from the mom to the growing baby—just like a lifeline takes oxygen to an astronaut when he or she is doing a spacewalk—and then takes waste from the baby and returns it to the mom to get rid of. When a baby is born, that connection isn't needed anymore since the baby will breathe on its own and get nutrition in other ways, so the umbilical cord gets cut, leaving the baby with a **belly button** to remember it by.

Where do other sperm go after one gets chosen to be the baby? If another sperm gets in, will that make twins?

Once a *single sperm* gets into an egg, another sperm cannot. It just can't happen, because that would create too many **genes** to make a person. (For more on twins, see page 98 on the girls' side.) Meanwhile, any extra sperm die.

Is a pregnant man possible?

You have to have a **uterus** to get pregnant, which usually means you have to be born biologically **female**.

Is it possible for a gay couple to have a baby?

Since an egg and a sperm are needed to start a baby, and a uterus is needed to grow one, two guys can't biologically have a baby with each other, but there are several other ways they can **become parents**. They can *adopt* a baby, or one of them can have a baby with a woman (by *donating* his sperm) and then raise that baby. A guy can get together with or marry another guy who already has a child and become a *stepdad*. Or sometimes a guy will have married a woman and already had children, but then realize he is gay and get together with a man—he's already a dad and will continue to be one with his new partner. If the gay couple is made up of *two women*, one of them can get pregnant with sperm from a donor.

. . . .

So, in the end, I'm just a sperm, right?

You are way, **way more** than a sperm. You are a boy growing up—that means you are an amazing human being who is embarking on an exciting expedition to **dis-cover life**. You are a *thinking, feeling person*. You are a son, grandson, friend, student, perhaps a brother, and, for sure, a normal person growing up. You will become a **man**—*wow, imagine that*. You will notice changes in yourself and changes all around you as you grow. You'll have the opportunity to make a zillion **choices** about where you want to go and what you want to do. And, if you choose, you can be a parent yourself one day and perhaps help your son (or daughter) to successfully complete this same **growing-up** trip that you're going through right now.

Why do some people think they are ANOTHER GENDER when they are actually not?

Gender means the way someone expresses themselves as masculine (male) or feminine (female). In our culture most people used to think gender was determined by the reproductive parts you were born with. Now we know things are *more complicated*. Someone's **brain** can feel male or female or somewhere in between, regardless of the **biological parts** they're born with. Since most people will treat a child as a boy if they have a penis or a girl if they have a vagina, it can be totally confusing for someone whose brain is telling them something different. And it can take some time for these kids to figure out what is going on.

I've heard that if you have sex on a certain day it will affect whether you have a boy or girl.

Throughout history, people have wondered what determines the sex of a baby—whether it will be a boy or a girl. Someone's sex is determined by what reproductive parts they are born with. Generally, it has nothing to do with the day you have sex, what you eat, what you're thinking, or what you're wearing before you have sex. Half of the dad's sperm carry an "X" chromosome and half carry the "Y" chromosome. Whichever sperm happens to get to the egg first *determines which sex the baby will be*. The mom's egg has nothing to do with the sex of the baby, since all eggs have the "X" chromosome. If a "Y"-carrying sperm combines with an egg, it makes an "XY," which will be a boy. If an "X"-carrying sperm combines with an egg, then it's a girl, or "XX."

But there's more to the gender story. In our culture, most people used to think the reproductive parts a baby is born with tell us absolutely if it's a boy or girl. However, we now know there's another important part of one's body regarding gender—*their brain*. A person's brain will tell that person, "I feel I am a boy" or "I feel I am a girl" or "I feel like I'm some of both." For most babies, the brain matches the reproductive parts—boy brain with boy parts or girl brain with girl parts. But for some babies, the brain and the reproductive parts don't match—they could be a boy brain with girl parts or a girl brain with boy parts. Someone born this way may call themselves *trans or transgender*. Scientists and doctors are still learning a lot about what our brains tell us about our gender. Sometimes it can be really hard or confusing for kids growing up who realize they're transgender. If you feel like your parts don't match how your brain feels, or you're just not sure what your brain is telling you about who you are or who you're attracted to, it's important to talk to a trusted adult to help you figure it all out.

15. Why Don't Men Talk About **Feelings** and **Emotions?**

. . . And Other Questions About Friends, Feelings, and Worries

Is it better to be different or like everyone else?

That's a great question! When you're growing up, you usually want to feel **included**. This means you try to be interested in what others are interested in, or you pick similar clothes, or you pick the same music, *all because you want others to like you*. But as you get older, you might feel like you want to be an **individual**, and like you want to be treated as the **unique** person you are. What drives adults crazy is that teenagers can feel these two things at exactly the same time! *Even grown-ups sometimes* want to fit in and at other times want to do their own thing.

What do I look like when you look at me? (What do other people see in me?)

It is totally **normal** for people to wonder what other people think of them. They may ask themselves, "Am I normal?" Or, "Am I like the others?" There are things about each of us that are the **same** as others—we all have a brain and a heart. There are also things about each of us that might be a little **different**—we have different personalities, different likes and dislikes, and different appearances. *That's a good thing.* We want to feel like we **fit in**; at the same time, we might *not want* to look and sound *exactly* like everyone else. Teenagers often worry about how they're seen by others. The truth is, *it's normal to wonder this*—adults do too.

. . . .

Why are people shunned by others if they're not exactly alike?

All people want to be part of a group that **accepts** them and treats them well. Sometimes people will try to make a group more **exclusive** by not letting others into the group. They think that rejecting others will make them feel more **important**. Unfortunately, this can result in making others feel bad. Being rejected can happen to everyone at some point. That's OK—*there are plenty of other people* who would be thrilled to have you in their group.

. . . .

At what age does one become bitter and hateful?

Yikes! That's quite a question! Most people are kind, loving, and full of hope and other good things. Sometimes, if someone is having a **hard time**—because of **stress**, financial issues, abuse, or unfair things done to them during their lives—they can come across as *mean or irritable*. Everyone has bad days, for sure, but most people are generally **good**, and they *stay that way their whole lives.*

Do your feelings for family and friends change during ages ten to twenty?

Our **feelings** can definitely **change** as we get older. Even though we can love our families forever, the ways we interact depend on our age and our **experiences** with each other. Many of us think back to friends we used to know and liked a lot but who are no longer active in our lives. We change; they change. *That's part of growing up.*

. . . .

Is it normal to feel EMBARRASSED with your mom there when your friends are around?

It is **normal** for teens to want to spend more time with their friends as they get older. Some teens might be concerned that being seen with family will make others think they're less "**grown up.**" But the adults you live with still have a big job to do *helping you* grow up during those years. They still want to keep you safe, help you when you're in trouble, and share your good times. Even though some boys think they should **distance** themselves from their mother to act more like a grown man, some feel more comfortable talking over things with their mom, while others feel more at ease with their dad. Parents are really *important guides* to help you through those teen years, and each can help you in different ways.

Will I get more STRESS when I get older?

Stress comes in all shapes and sizes. It can be **bad**, such as being mugged on the street by a robber, or actually **good**, such as when you push yourself to play harder at soccer to win the championship. It can come from *others*, like when your parents ask you repeatedly to clean up your room and don't let you use the computer until you do, or from *yourself*, such as when you get down on yourself for missing a question on a test. And stress can be **different** depending on your age—for a kid it could be trying to fit in with your friends, while for a grown-up it could be getting a good job. Stress is something that *all people* face throughout their lives. Part of growing up is learning how to handle stress in the best way possible. Parents or other trusted adults can share with you the ways they have learned to deal with stress so you don't feel **overwhelmed**.

Is it normal to fear responsibilities?

It is normal to **wonder** what's in store for you and even to **worry** about whether you'll *be able to handle it all*. But having **responsibilities** goes right along with having **privileges**—they're part of growing up. Your family, school, and community are getting you ready to handle these responsibilities when you're an adult. Try asking people in your family whether they were worried about responsibilities when they were young and how they overcame those worries.

Who defines COOL?

That's a very *hard question* to answer! **Cool** is basically defined by **groups** of people. If enough people (especially people others admire) think something is cool, the rest might go along with it and think so too. As a silly example, imagine that a famous rock group decides to wear their shorts over their heads. If you see other boys

doing the same thing, you might think that wearing shorts in that way must be cool. What is cool **changes** constantly, depending on *fads and what's popular*. Everyone at your age wants to fit in and feel important, so it's OK to want to be cool. Try asking your family how they tried to be cool at your age.

Is DEPRESSION common during puberty?

Everyone feels **sad** or **lonely** every so often—*that's normal*. Sometimes it can be pretty bad after losing someone important to you or if you've had a great **disappointment**. But if you find you're feeling sad, lonely, or hopeless a lot of the time, or all the time, then that's *not OK*. It's time to let someone know so they can help you feel better. You can start by sharing with an adult you trust. There are also lots of professionals who are specially trained to help kids who are feeling bad about themselves. Occasionally this can get so bad that a person might think it's not worth living anymore—this is a definite time to let someone know. There are lots of things they can do and suggest that will make things **feel better** for you.

. . . .

On advertisements, they put pretty women on the ad. What message are they sending?

Ads are made to sell you things. Advertisers know that they need to get your **attention** to make you want to buy their products. So sometimes they will use something they think you'll like, and **associate** it with the product they're selling. For example, certain sports drinks are advertised with famous athletes—that's so you'll think that drinking the sports drink will make you look or perform like that athlete. Advertisers will even use things in their advertisements that have nothing to do with the products they're selling—like a pretty woman in a car commercial. They think that if you get a **good feeling** about the woman, you'll also have a good feeling about the car and want to buy one. *Even adults fall for this trick.* Your question is a great one to talk with your family about—what **messages** are television programs, movies, and ads sending you about growing up?

What is the point of a porno movie?

Pornography is something in books, photographs, or videos that shows men's and women's bodies acting in a sexual way. Some people take an interest in these pictures as a way to live out *the sexual thoughts they are having.* One problem with this, however, is that in many places it is illegal (for instance, to send sexual pictures through cell phones or mail to a different state, to include pictures of kids or teens, or if there are laws against sexual pictures where you live). Another problem with pornography is that some of the people in these pictures are treated unfairly or even hurt. The stories and the bodies of the actors in porn are often unrealistic. Porn often shows people experiencing sex being done *to* them—not *with* each other in an equally respectful relationship. So pornography is not helpful in learning how to build healthy sexual relationships. You will inevitably come across pornography, and it is normal to feel curious about it. We know that watching pornography does *not* help people grow up to understand themselves as sexual people or how to be in healthy relationships—in fact, the opposite. To be a healthy sexual person means *taking care of your body* and learning from your family and books like this about being in real sexual relationships.

. . . .

Why don't men talk about FEELINGS AND EMOTIONS?

Some men don't talk as much about their feelings because they're taught not to in many cultures and families. In some cases, a boy's image of a man is someone who keeps his feelings to himself and doesn't let his emotions be obvious to others. This may not be the case in your family. What do you think characterizes a man? What should a man look like? How should he act? How should he behave around others? What's his role in a family or in his community? There are no easy answers to these questions, and people have very different opinions about what men should be like. This would be a great thing to *talk with your family* about. Maybe their opinions changed as they got older themselves.

How do I ask my PARENTS about things that they might not like?

When you're **young**, parents might make most of the decisions because you don't yet have the experience and maturity to do so. *As you get older,* there is usually more sharing in decision-making, and when you're mostly grown up, more and more decisions are made by you. When you start to make **decisions** together, you'll share what you think and *listen to their thoughts* in return. They won't like everything you say, but they'll be glad you talked to them so you can decide **together**.

. . . .

When do I get STRICT like Dad?

One of a parent's main jobs is to keep their kids **safe**. They usually do this in the best way they know how. This can seem strict to you as a kid because you might hear about friends who are allowed to do things you are not. Some of us grown-ups remember our parents as being **strict** when we were kids, but we realize now that they were just trying to keep us safe. Also some parents come from different traditions that don't permit kids to do certain things, like date, so they are *less familiar* and therefore more **cautious**. As a teenager, you will hopefully have more opportunities to talk these things over with the grown-ups you live with so everyone *understands each other* better.

Can you not have PEER PRESSURE?

A peer is a *friend or classmate*, so when they are pushing you to do something scary, unsafe, or in some way uncomfortable for you, that's peer pressure. Peer pressure can also be good, like when a friend **encourages** you to try harder to win a race, and you do. Sometimes you can easily resist peer pressure, like when someone dares you to do something you know you don't want to. And sometimes it's **hard to resist**. Another kind of peer pressure actually comes from inside you, such as when you see kids at school wearing the latest, cool running shoes, and you think if you also get a pair you will feel cool or be more popular. No one *told* you to get those shoes so the pressure is actually coming from inside yourself. We face many types of **peer pressure** our whole lives—some are good and some are not, some are easy to resist and some are not. We all want to **belong** and be included with interesting, cool people—the key is figuring out whether pressure is good or bad and coming up with ways to deal with it when it happens.

Thanks. You've answered all my questions.

Although this might have been *more information* than you expected, you will be coming up with many, many more **questions** as you grow up, for sure. This is because you gain *new experiences* that make you see things differently and because that brain of yours will be **changing** and making new questions pop up into your head. There are many good places to help you figure things out, such as reliable internet sites, teachers, health-care providers, and all the other trusted adults in your life. And keep on **reading** for ideas on how to start conversations with others to become comfortable talking about these things and asking all the new growing-up questions you **discover**!

What I Wish My Parents Understood About Kids

- We like to stay up late

- How tired we are

- I wish they understood how we don't get tired at nine thirty, we get tired at ten

- Sometimes we like to hang out with our friends and not our parents

- The importance of video-gaming

- We don't want to be treated like a little kid

- We need privacy

- That we do listen

- That we feel stressed out too and that sometimes we need to quit an activity if we don't like it anymore

- We don't always want parents to ask how school was that day